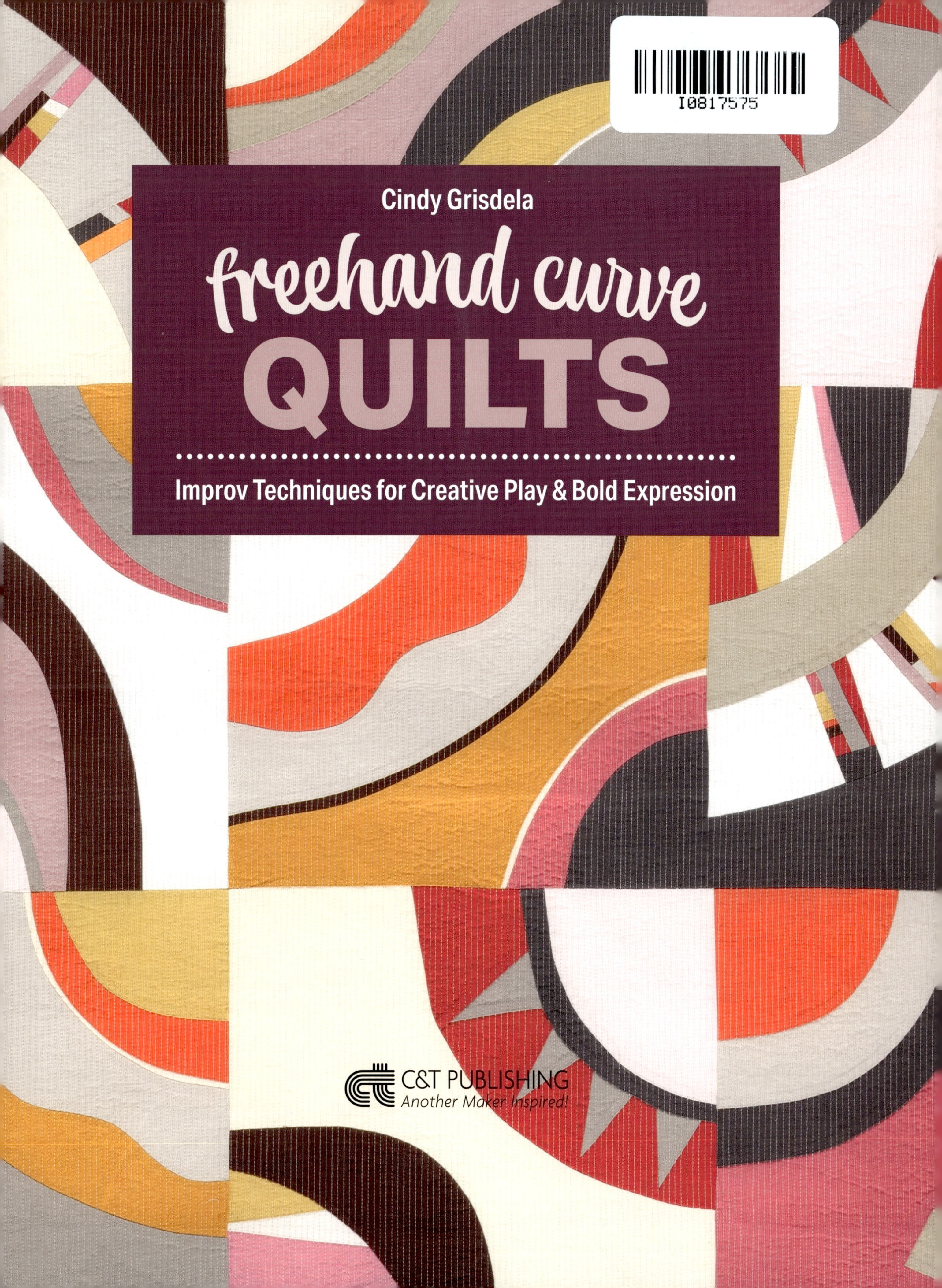
I0817575
Cindy Grisdela
freehand curve
QUILTS
Improv Techniques for Creative Play & Bold Expression
C&T PUBLISHING
Another Maker Inspired!

Text and photography copyright © 2026
by Cindy Grisdela

Photography and artwork copyright © 2026 by C&T Publishing, Inc.

Publisher: Amy Barrett-Daffin

Creative Director: Gailen Runge

Senior Editor: Roxane Cerda

Editor: Gailen Runge

Technical Editor: Debbie Rodgers

Cover/Book Designer: April Mostek

Production Coordinator: Tim Manibusan

Illustrator: Aliza Shalit

Photography Coordinator: Rachel Ackley

Photography by C&T Publishing,
unless otherwise noted

All rights reserved. No part of this work covered by the copyright hereon may be used in any form or reproduced by any means—graphic, electronic, or mechanical, including photocopying, recording, taping, or information storage and retrieval systems—without written permission from the publisher. The copyrights on individual artworks are retained by the artists as noted in *Freehand Curve Quilts*. These designs may be used to make items for personal use only and may not be used for the purpose of personal profit. Items created to benefit nonprofit groups, or that will be publicly displayed, must be conspicuously labeled with the following credit: "Designs copyright © 2026 by Cindy Grisdela from the book *Freehand Curve Quilts* from C&T Publishing, Inc." Permission for all other purposes must be requested in writing from C&T Publishing, Inc.

Attention Teachers: C&T Publishing, Inc., encourages the use of our books as texts for teaching. You can find lesson plans for many of our titles at ctpub.com or contact us at ctinfo@ctpub.com.

We take great care to ensure that the information included in our products is accurate and presented in good faith, but no warranty is provided, nor are results guaranteed. Having no control over the choices of materials or procedures used, neither the author nor C&T Publishing, Inc., shall have any liability to any person or entity with respect to any loss or damage caused directly or indirectly by the information contained in this book. For your convenience, we post an up-to-date listing of corrections on our website (ctpub.com). If a correction is not already noted, please contact our customer service department at ctinfo@ctpub.com or P.O. Box 1456, Lafayette, CA 94549.

Trademark (™) and registered trademark (®) names are used throughout this book. Rather than use the symbols with every occurrence of a trademark or registered trademark name, we are using the names only in the editorial fashion and to the benefit of the owner, with no intention of infringement.

Library of Congress Cataloging-in-Publication Data

Names: Grisdela, Cindy, 1958- author

Title: Freehand curve quilts : improv techniques for creative play & bold expression / by Cindy Grisdela.

Description: Lafayette, CA : C&T Publishing, [2026] | Summary: "Take your creativity to the next level with Improv curves cut freehand-no patterns or templates needed. Use your rotary cutter as a drawing tool to create curves, then personalize them with confetti pops, skinny lines, wonky triangles, fried egg curves, and more. Guided exercises help you combine techniques into an original design"-- Provided by publisher.

Identifiers: LCCN 2025026297 | ISBN 9781644036525 trade paperback | ISBN 9781644036532 ebook

Subjects: LCSH: Quilting--Patterns | Patchwork quilts | Directional stitching | Improvisation in art

Classification: LCC TT835 .G765425 2026 | DDC 746.46/041--dc23/eng/20250610

LC record available at https://lccn.loc.gov/2025026297

Printed in China

10 9 8 7 6 5 4 3 2 1

dedication

To my family, as always. I wouldn't be who I am without your love and support.

acknowledgments

I wasn't sure I wanted to write another book, but I ran into Gailen Runge, Creative Director at C&T Publishing, at QuiltCon in 2024 and she asked me if I had thought about it. Each book teaches me something, and I had learned a lot from the first two. Plus, my students were starting to ask when the next book was coming out, so I decided to give it another shot and focus on curves, which I've been playing with in one form or another over my entire quilting journey. Thank you, Gailen, for giving me the push I needed.

I am indebted to the entire staff at C&T for giving me the opportunity to fulfill a long-held dream of being an author with *Artful Improv* in 2015. Special thanks to Amy Barrett-Daffin, C&T's Publisher, and April Mostek, who designed all three of my books.

For being my sounding boards, critique group, and all-around friends, who give me support when I need it and a kick when I need that, many thanks to Susan Lapham, Maureen Melville, Maria Shell, Heather Pregger, Irene Roderick, Avice Meehan, Robin Jones, and Melissa Frumin.

Thanks to all the students who have taken my classes online and in person over the last 10 years—-you are the best! Special thanks to Sherrill Ash, Nina Clotfelter, Angela Gubler, Candi Lennox, and Linda Hungerford for sharing their Fabulous Freehand Curves quilts for this book.

I am grateful to e bond (Free Spirit Fabrics) for designing wonderful fabrics that reignited my love of prints, some of which are in the projects in this book, and to John Tsiaperas of Flourish Quilts for longarm quilting *Curves Around* and *Any Which Way* in time so they could be included in the book.

Finally, thanks to my family—my husband Phil for believing in me and supporting my journey, Phil and Matt for their encouragement of Mom's dream, siblings Margaret, Ben, and Allen for being there when I need them, and my parents Eleanor and Ben Samuels for their lifelong love and support of my desire to be an artist.

contents

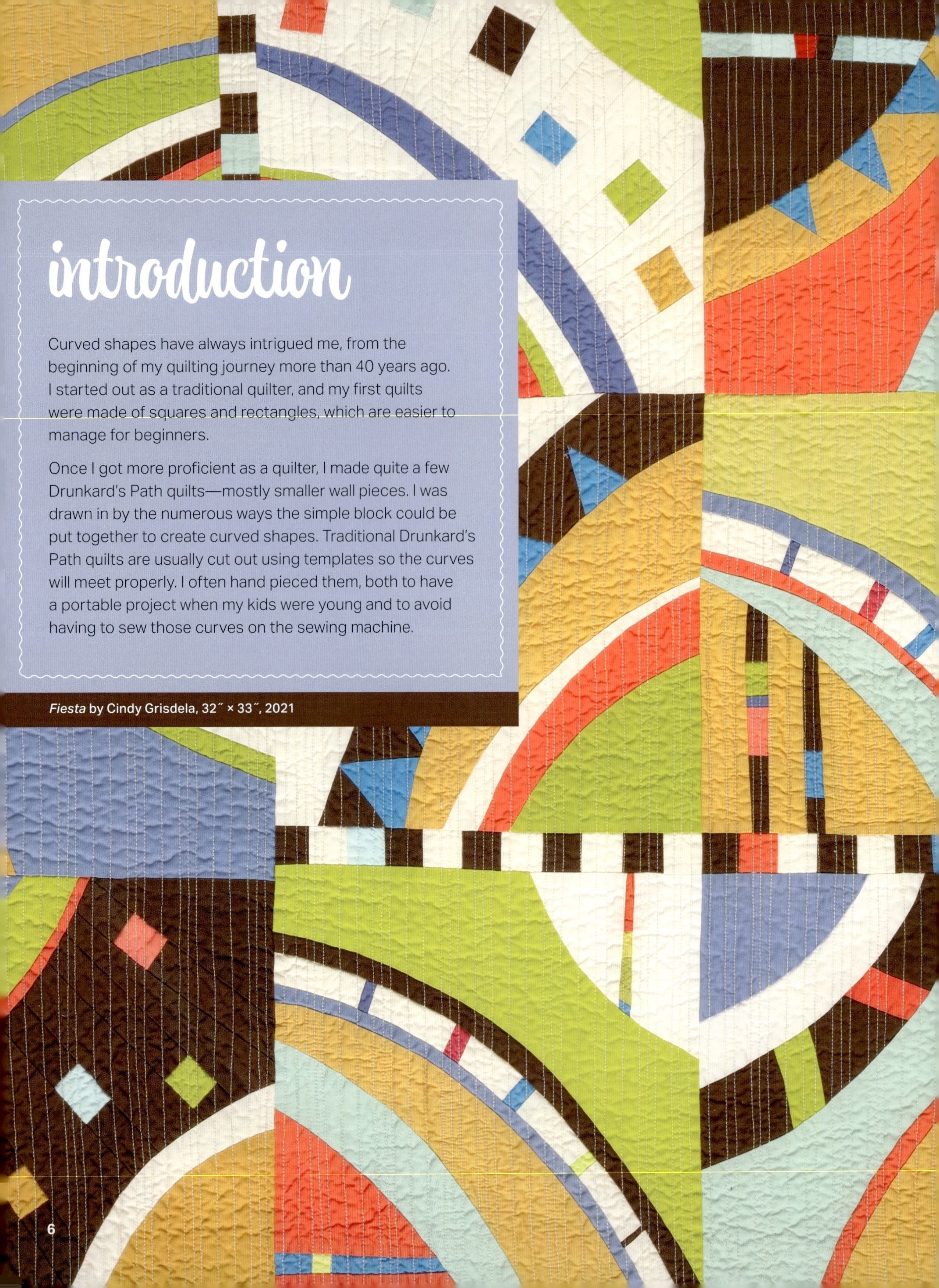

introduction

Curved shapes have always intrigued me, from the beginning of my quilting journey more than 40 years ago. I started out as a traditional quilter, and my first quilts were made of squares and rectangles, which are easier to manage for beginners.

Once I got more proficient as a quilter, I made quite a few Drunkard's Path quilts—mostly smaller wall pieces. I was drawn in by the numerous ways the simple block could be put together to create curved shapes. Traditional Drunkard's Path quilts are usually cut out using templates so the curves will meet properly. I often hand pieced them, both to have a portable project when my kids were young and to avoid having to sew those curves on the sewing machine.

Fiesta by Cindy Grisdela, 32″ × 33″, 2021

Around the Mill Pond (right) was one of those quilts—pieced and quilted by hand using an autumn color palette inspired by the cabinets and countertops I used in a kitchen renovation around that time. The setting is traditional.

Around the Mill Pond by Cindy Grisdela, 25″ × 25″, 2006

Splash of Color by Cindy Grisdela, 21″ × 27″, 2009

Splash of Color (left) was made a few years later, hand pieced and free motion quilted. I chose batiks in black and white and the colors of the color wheel to make an original design, moving from red in the upper left through yellow, green, blue, and purple, and then back to red.

As I began to explore more contemporary designs, I wondered if curved shapes could be cut without templates, and I came up with what I called Improv Curves in *Artful Improv* and *Adventures in Improv Quilts*. Stacking fabrics and cutting curves freehand resulted in interesting shapes that could be arranged in different ways to create new quilts.

Neon Fizz II (right) is a good example of this technique. I liked the way the curves didn't match on the edges like they would in a traditional Drunkard's Path design, giving the design visual texture and energy. But the stacking technique had significant limitations. I had little control over the way the curves interacted with each other, and I couldn't change the order of the colors once they were stacked and cut.

Neon Fizz II by Cindy Grisdela, 25″ × 25″, 2021.

ask what if?

"What If?" is one of the most powerful questions in my Improv toolkit. It's the start of all the best ideas. Of course, the first idea doesn't always work or turn out to be the greatest idea, but ideas generate ideas. Then I start cutting and sewing to see what will happen. If you prefer to draw your ideas on paper or use a computer program first, that's a perfectly valid way to explore new options.

> *"What If?" is one of the most powerful questions in my Improv toolkit. It's the start of all the best ideas.*

But I'm an intuitive, organic artist and I love the feel and texture of fabric, so I usually just dive right in.

What if I created each block individually, so I would have control over the colors in the block, the elements I choose to add to make it my own, and how each block interacts with the ones around it? This is the freehand curve technique. It's not my invention, but I have used the technique to make designs that are unique to me.

Sunny Side Up by Cindy Grisdela, 36″ × 50″, 2020

Sunny Side Up, the first quilt I made using these ideas, was not as successful as I had hoped. Part of the problem was the odd color palette I chose, and part was that I just didn't have very interesting lines and shapes. I ended up stacking two blocks on top of each other right sides up, cutting them in half diagonally, then swapping the halves and sewing them back together. I also quilted a variety of free-motion motifs in the different shapes of the quilt, which helped, too. Although the first try wasn't amazing, I still believed in the idea and decided to explore it further.

This is one of the joys and frustrations of Improv design. Because you don't have a pattern to tell you the steps, things don't always work out at first. But if the idea is interesting, I keep trying to see if I can create a design that makes my heart sing. I share these less than stellar beginnings so you can see that disappointment in not being able to make the idea in your head work happens to all of us, even someone like me who works at it every day as my job.

Fiesta by Cindy Grisdela, 32″ × 33″, 2021

I was happier with *Fiesta*. The color palette had a southwestern feel that I liked and by asking "what if?" I came up with the idea of adding more compelling lines and shapes to each block. Design elements you'll learn about in this book—insets, wonky triangles, and confetti pops—all added to the composition in a positive way.

By now, I've made a variety of freehand-curve quilts, experimenting with color palettes, components, sizes, and design elements. The technique lends itself to wall quilts, baby quilts, and even functional bed quilts by varying the size and number of the blocks. Your blocks can be relatively simple and unadorned, use multiple components, or anywhere in between.

For this book, I wanted to take a deep dive into this technique—curves cut freehand without patterns or templates. Together we will explore different ways to use the rotary cutter like a drawing tool to craft appealing curved lines and shapes and then embellish them with all kinds of fun components, such as pieced insets, curved overlays, and skinny lines.

This is an Improv process without patterns or templates, so you'll be making your own decisions about color, line, and shape as you work through the techniques and guided exercises in this book. These techniques are accessible to everyone, even if you don't have much experience with curves. Working with large blocks is easier than smaller ones and the blocks are oversized so they can be trimmed down when finished.

As you create, silence your inner critic and let your inner child come out to play!

Not every block, or quilt for that matter, will be a masterpiece, and that's okay. Start with smaller projects and learn from blocks that aren't your favorites. What did you like about it? What didn't work and how can you apply that lesson to the next one?

Grab your rotary cutter and let's get started!

My sewing studio on the lake. I piece with a Juki TL-2010Q and do free-motion stitching with a Bernina Q20.

Photo by Cindy Grisdela

where to start

No templates, no patterns, and no rules—that's my Improv process of creating with freehand cut curves. Of course you can decide on a few guidelines to help you define your project if you wish—I usually do. Just be open to making changes as the design takes shape.

Full Wild by Cindy Grisdela, 52″ × 54″, 2023

You can use only simple curves, or curves and wonky triangles, or add confetti pops and skinny lines to your composition. It's all up to you.

One decision is made for us here, because we're going to be designing with freehand cut curves. The next decisions to make in the process are what fabrics to use—solids, prints, or a combination—and what mood you want to convey in the colors that you choose.

Twist and Shout by Cindy Grisdela, 46″ × 48″, 2022
Simple curves, insets, wonky triangles, confetti pops, and more in the same design.

fabric

Fabric is our paint; the raw material we use to design our creations. Each of us has favorite fabrics we like to use as we create. Maybe it's patterned batiks or other commercial prints, or maybe it's solid fabrics. Any of these will work in this process, alone or in combination.

I moved away from using print fabrics in my work a number of years ago because I felt solid fabrics conveyed a more graphic element in my work. The lines and shapes are more distinct than they are with print fabrics and the look is more contemporary to my eye. Sometimes with print fabrics it's not clear whether the eye should focus on the lines and shapes I've created, or the lines and shapes printed on the fabric. That's my choice, but feel free to use the fabrics that you love to make your quilts your own.

Any Which Way by Cindy Grisdela, 38″ × 39″, 2024
Solid fabrics focus the eye on the lines and shapes in the design.

Recently I've started to add print fabrics back into my work, mostly as an accent or contrast.

For *Full Wild* (right), I started with fat quarters from the ROOT fabric line designed by e bond for Free Spirit Fabrics. Something about the strong colors and graphic shapes in the fabrics inspired me. I combined the prints with a variety of solids using the easy multiple cut curves technique detailed in Using Leftovers (page 57) and I was thrilled with how well they worked together in the design.

Full Wild by Cindy Grisdela, 52″ × 54″, 2023

Improv Curves is a stacking technique that creates blocks in sets. Each block has one print fabric and three, or sometimes four, solids that coordinate with that print. I didn't plan it out ahead of time, just made one set of blocks at a time. Because I was using a specific line of print fabric, I was fairly sure that the blocks would work together once completed.

As I was designing the quilt, I made up some rules to guide me as I went. The blocks were cut with two curves in one corner and one curve in the opposite corner. I made one set with 5 fabrics then I decided I liked the blocks with only four fabrics instead of five, because the print showed up better. I used that set in the composition, but didn't make any more that way.

I set the blocks so the two curves going in the same direction formed a complete circle and the corners with a single curve formed another circle. The circles are staggered in the design vertically, so they aren't all in the same row. If you look at the top of the quilt, you'll see that every row begins with a half circle to accomplish that staggered look.

In each circle, there is only one print fabric. Using those guidelines, the quilt emerged. This is a maximalist design with a lot of energy. But the orderliness of the staggered rows and the guideline to have only one print fabric in each circle ensure that the print fabrics are distributed somewhat evenly around the design and helps to bring some calm to the overall composition.

Baby Blues by Cindy Grisdela, 20″ × 20″, 2024
Photo by Cindy Grisdela

Blue Eyes by Cindy Grisdela, 52″ × 53″, 2023

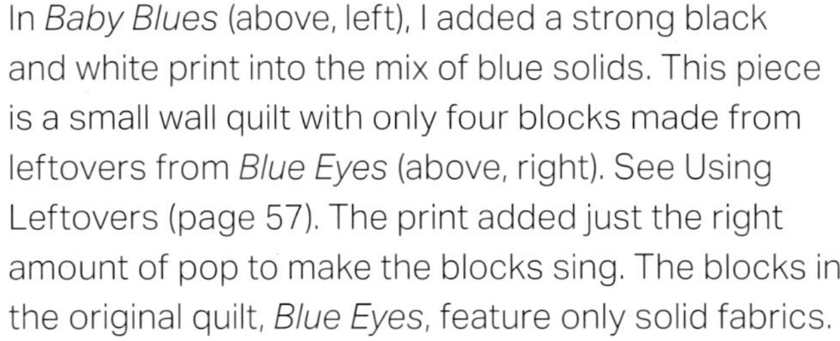

In *Baby Blues* (above, left), I added a strong black and white print into the mix of blue solids. This piece is a small wall quilt with only four blocks made from leftovers from *Blue Eyes* (above, right). See Using Leftovers (page 57). The print added just the right amount of pop to make the blocks sing. The blocks in the original quilt, *Blue Eyes*, feature only solid fabrics.

Neither choice is right or wrong—prints or solids. Use the fabrics that speak to you as an artist. I do recommend that if you primarily use prints in your designs that you try to include some fabrics that are low volume, tone on tone, or "read" as solids for contrast.

color and value

For freehand curve designs, I usually choose 9–13 fat quarters in colors I like together. Often, I start with a mood or energy I want to convey. Warm colors like red, orange, and yellow communicate energy and light, like sunlight or fire, while cool colors like green, blue, and purple are usually calmer and more serene, like the sky or a still lake.

I choose 6–8 fabrics to be the base of the design—either warm or cool colors depending on the mood I want. Then I choose 2–3 fabrics that are different in value or intensity for a pop of contrast, and 1–2 fabrics that read as dull if my overall palette is on the bright side, or that read as bright if my palette is more muted.

Those last 3–5 fabrics will be used in smaller proportions relative to the base colors.

It's important to choose a mix of values—light, medium, and dark, as well as a range of colors. The variety in value gives visual depth to the design that isn't possible when you use only medium values, for example. The saying "Color gets all the credit but value does all the work." may be a cliche, but it's a useful thought to keep in mind as you choose fabrics for your quilt.

If you want to add more diversity to your fabric choices, consider adding a new value of one or more of your colors—either lighter or darker—rather than adding more colors to the mix.

Supernova (right) was inspired by the idea of fire and light, so I used bright, warm colors on a black background. The base of the design is red, red orange, and red purple. Bright yellow, lime green, and turquoise are the contrasts, and the black, dull burgundy, and gold are the lower intensity colors that allow the brights to pop.

Blue Eyes (page 13) has a calmer vibe with a wide range of blues, from turquoise to blue green, blue to blue purple. The values also range from light cornflower blue to dark navy. The contrast in this design is the black and white, and there are several dark blues and a gray that read as dull values.

Supernova by Cindy Grisdela, 40″ × 54″, 2023

'70s Serpentine by Cindy Grisdela, 54″ × 54″, 2025

'70s Serpentine has a color palette that reminds me of the colors surrounding me growing up in the '60s and '70s in Florida—avocado green, turquoise, gold, off white, and warm pink. These colors were often used in kitchens and bathrooms. There are several values of each color. For example, I used three values of red orange, and three values of blue, including one deep blue that has a lower saturation and two different turquoise blues that are brighter. There are also two values of olive green—one darker and one a little lighter for contrast.

Adding new values in the palette I'm working with adds interest to the design, rather than adding new colors to the mix and risking a carnival appearance. Of course, color choice is a personal decision and each of us has different preferences and different tolerances for energy in our work. Choose the palette that works for you.

CHOOSE A PRINT

One simple way to choose a color palette is to use a print fabric you like as inspiration.

This Kaffe Fassett print, *Persimmon Red*, is a favorite (Rowan Westminster Fabrics). By studying it carefully, it's clear that there are about 9 different colors used—two values of pink, two values of orange, two values of green, and two values of brown, plus a dull raisin purple in the background. The colors in the fabric are also a combination of bright saturated colors and duller versions.

Kaffe Fassett print *Persimmon Red*

Color palette inspired by the print fabric

Wonky Stripes by Cindy Grisdela, 27″ × 31″, 2023

Photo by Cindy Grisdela

I created *Wonky Stripes* (above) out of the solid fabrics I chose inspired by the Kaffe Fassett print, using Angled Stripe units (page 43) cut into various widths. I decided not to use the print in the composition, but there's no reason you couldn't do that if you wanted to.

Consider the proportion of each color in the original fabric design. I used all the colors in the print in relatively equal amounts in my design. Looking at the composition, it's apparent that the lime green is a strong value that pops when used in the same proportion as the rest of the colors. The lime green in the fabric itself is used sparingly, so the effect is more muted. The base colors in the fabric are the oranges, the pinks, and the pear green. If you wanted to make a quilt that was more true to the fabric design, you would probably limit the lime green to a contrast here and there.

Using dull and bright colors together may seem counterintuitive, but the dull colors often provide a base for the brighter colors to really pop. The contrast is what makes it work. If you use only dull colors, the design may seem flat, and if you only use bright colors, sometimes you end up with a "circus has come to town" effect. Using dulls and brights together allows both to play an important role in creating a compelling design.

In *Any Which Way* (page 39), I used a range of pinks from bright pink to a dull rose, along with orange, off white, and cinnamon brown. The dull brown, taupe, and charcoal gray in the palette temper the pinks in the design to keep it from being too sweet.

I've covered color extensively in my previous books—*Artful Improv* and *Adventures in Improv Quilts*—for a more indepth look at the subject.

tools

You don't need a lot of fancy tools or equipment for Improv quiltmaking, but having the right tool or equipment for the job you want to do will help you focus on your art and do your best work. Below are a few of the tools that I find indispensable. Feel free to try the ones that work for you.

60MM ROTARY CUTTER

The rotary cutter is a must-have tool for freehand cut curves. Think of it as a drawing tool rather than a cutting implement and buy the best one you can afford. My favorite is the OLFA 60mm cutter with a straight handle. The larger blade gives you greater control of your drawing lines, especially on the larger curves. Remember to change the blade when it gets dull or nicked so your drawing flows freely without the aggravation of having to recut lines.

OLFA 60mm rotary cutter

SEWING MACHINE WITH ¼″ FOOT

A fancy sewing machine isn't necessary for Improv quilting. All you need is the ability to sew a consistent ¼″ seam. I invest in the ¼″ foot that fits my machine. Some ¼″ feet come with a metal or plastic flange on the right side. I would avoid this feature because it makes it harder to sew curves accurately.

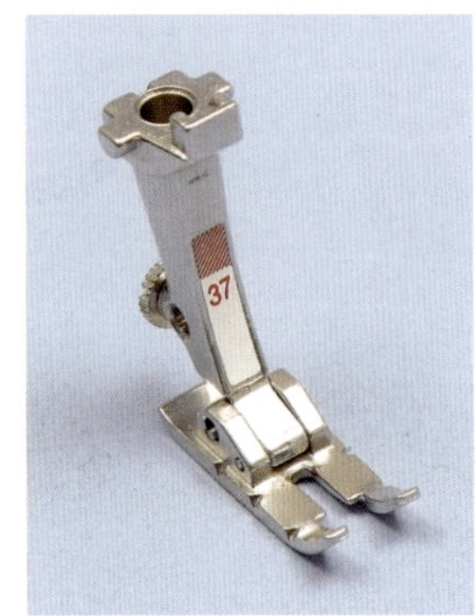

Bernina ¼″ foot

LARGE CUTTING MAT

A large cutting mat is essential to make the freehand curve process easier. I like the OLFA 24″ × 36″ self-healing mat, because it is large enough to work with the 15″ squares I like to use to begin cutting my curves and it doesn't dull my blades as quickly as some other options. You want to have plenty of room to cut your squares freely.

ROTARY CUTTING RULERS

I don't use rulers much in my work, but sometimes I need them. For this process, I like a 15″ square to cut my initial fabric squares and to trim the blocks once they are finished. A rectangular ruler is nice to have in addition to help with stabilizing the fabrics for Angled Stripes (page 43) and Confetti Pops (page 31). A 6″ × 12″ or 4″ × 14″ rectangle works for most jobs. I prefer the Omnigrid rulers with the yellow and black lines because the markings are easier to see for accurate cutting.

IRON AND IRONING SURFACE

I have a complicated relationship with irons. I've tried expensive ones and cheap ones, and never really found one that works for me. But an iron is crucial to make your seams lie flat, so make sure you have one that will do that for you, either with steam or with a spray bottle of water.

I like a large ironing board, so I have a Big Board pressing surface that lies on top of my fabric storage baskets. I use that one for ironing my blocks as I go. If I have a large quilt top, I might use a regular free-standing ironing board so the top doesn't get bunched up. I've also used wool pressing mats to get crisper seams.

DESIGN WALL

A design wall is almost as essential in my work as my sewing machine. As I'm making the blocks, I put them up on the wall so I can begin to see connections between them. I've found that if I make blocks independently without reference to the blocks around them, they are invariably less interesting.

A design wall can be as simple or elaborate as you wish. Anything from a piece of batting tacked up on the wall to a permanent fixture in your studio will work. If you don't have room for either of those, the floor or other horizontal surface can do the job, as long as you don't have pets or children that will disturb your work!

A design wall is useful to help see connections between your blocks.

Photo by Cindy Grisdela

My design wall is made up of 24″ × 24″ × 1″ squares of pink insulation board that I found at Home Depot. I taped them together with duct tape in several sections and covered the units with batting (flannel would work as well). The insulation board can be cut with a utility knife to fit your space or to make access to an electrical outlet on the wall. The units are attached to the wall with 3M Command Strips like those you would use for a dorm room. They can be removed without damaging the wall and you don't need any special tools to put them up.

I also have a moveable 36″ × 48″ design board that I made in the same way as my main design wall using three 24″ × 24″ × 1″ foam boards. I stacked two on top of each other and cut the other one in half and taped each half to one side of each square. This one provides an extra design surface if needed for a smaller project and it can be stored behind a door when not in use.

CAMERA

A camera is a useful tool to record your progress. As you design, you may want to try a variety of layouts for your blocks. Take a picture of each one so it can be recreated if you decide one of the first ideas was the best one. I usually just take snapshots on my phone—it doesn't have to be anything elaborate. It is also useful to use your camera's black and white filter to look at your composition to help you see if your values are falling where you want them.

Black and white photo of *Any Which Way* (page 39)

Quilt storage in a reclaimed cabinet.

Photo by Cindy Grisdela

techniques

On the following pages are the techniques I use most often to create my freehand curve quilts. Treat them as ideas to get you started on your own design path. Feel free to try them alone, in combination, or combined with ideas you come up with yourself.

I recommend that you work on a design wall (page 17) as you make your blocks, rather than working on them independently and then trying to put them together into a design. If you are able to see your blocks while you work, you'll make more striking connections between them in color and value, as well as in the elements you choose to include in each one.

As you finish each block, trim the edges to create the largest block possible (it doesn't have to be square). See Puzzling Blocks Together (page 38) for more suggestions.

For each technique, cut the curves *right sides up* and sew *right sides together* using a ¼″ seam.

Supernova by Cindy Grisdela, 40″ × 54″, 2023

SEWING CURVES

Sewing curves can be intimidating but it is far easier than some new to the technique expect. Improv cutting and piecing makes sewing curves even easier because there are no templates and no exact seam lines to be followed.

To sew a smooth seam, you will want to pin your pieces right sides together to help align them and sew slowly, adjusting the fullness of the concave (pizza crust) piece.

Find the Center and Pin

Before sewing two curved pieces, find and align the centers. To find the center of each curved element, gently fold the curve and finger press the center line. Or you can make a light registration mark within the seam allowance with a pencil.

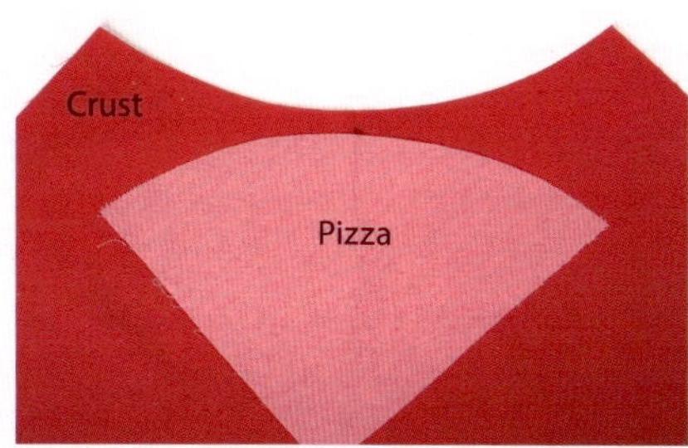

Finger press the center of each curve.

There is no definitive answer about which side should be on top—the concave (crust) or convex (pizza) side. I sew the seam with the convex/pizza piece on the bottom and the other piece on the top—I call it the crust to keep with the food metaphor. The crust piece has a bias edge and stretches more readily than the pizza piece. The only exception to this is if you are left-handed. I have found that many of my left-handed students find it works better to sew with the pizza on the top. Try it and see which way works best for you.

With the concave or crust piece on top, pin the pieces together every 1″ or so from the center out. Gently smooth the edge of the crust/concave piece so it runs along the edge of the pizza/convex piece and pin it in place. As you pin the pieces along the length, the already pinned crust will ruffle slightly. As you sew, this rufflling will smooth out.

Stitch slowly and stop when necessary to gently realign the edges.

Ears and Tails are Normal

You will have "ears" or "tails" on either end of your curves after you sew them. This is normal because you are taking up seam allowances as you sew. Don't try to match the edges of the curves or the block will have puckers or puffiness.

> ***Cut Blocks Larger***
> **To create 12½″–14″ blocks, cut 15″ or 16″ squares from your fat quarters or yardage. Or cut your initial blocks 3–4″ larger than you want your finished block to be.**

1. Choose 8–12 fabrics for your blocks. Refer to Where to Start (page 10) for suggestions on how to pick your colors. Remember to use a variety of values as well as a variety of colors. You may need another fat quarter of some of the fabrics, depending on the techniques you choose to use.

2. From your grouping, choose 2 fabrics you like together. Lay the blocks on top of one another on your cutting surface *right sides up* and cut a gentle upward curve through both layers, cutting a shape like a piece of pizza.

Cut a curved shape in one corner of your first pair of 15″ × 15″ squares.

3. Choose one combination of the 2 fabrics to sew together. Put the other pieces aside to use later.

4. Cut a new curve, the crust, from the second fabric to attach to your pizza shape.

5. Sew the first 2 curves together. Starting from the center, with right sides together, pin along the curve about 1″ apart along the entire curve. Stitch with a ¼″ seam, aiming for a smooth curve.

Ears and tails are normal.

simple freehand curves

The basic block has only curved elements that vary in color, value, and shape. Start with one of these blocks to get used to cutting your curves freehand. Think about using your rotary cutter as a drawing tool to create beautiful curved lines and shapes. I often cut my curves standing up so I can put my whole upper body into the curve. If it helps you to visualize your shapes, draw a few blocks on sketch paper first.

1. Choose 8–12 fabrics for your blocks. Refer to Where to Start (page 10) for suggestions on how to pick your colors. Remember to use a variety of values as well as a variety of colors. You may need another fat quarter of some of the fabrics, depending on the techniques you choose to use.

2. From your grouping, choose 2 fabrics you like together. Lay the blocks on top of one another on your cutting surface *right sides up* and cut a gentle upward curve through both layers, cutting a shape like a piece of pizza.

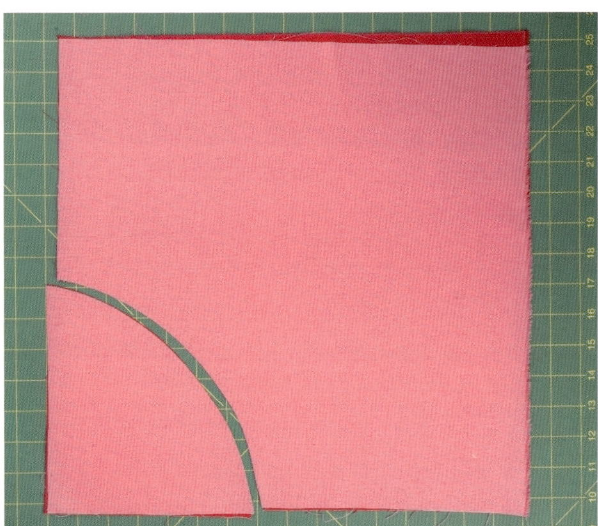

Cut a curved shape in one corner of your first pair of 15″ × 15″ squares.

3. Choose one combination of the 2 fabrics to sew together. Put the other pieces aside to use later.

4. Cut a new curve, the crust, from the second fabric to attach to your pizza shape.

5. Sew the first 2 curves together. Starting from the center, with right sides together, pin along the curve about 1″ apart along the entire curve. Stitch with a ¼″ seam, aiming for a smooth curve. For more advice on sewing curves, see Sewing Curves, page 21.

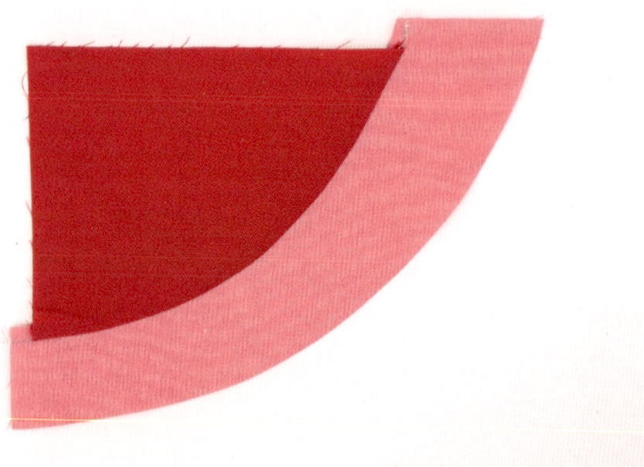

6. Press the seam toward the pizza shape.

7. Lay the completed unit on top of a third fabric *right sides up* and cut the new fabric along the outer curve you just sewed so the curves will fit together when you sew them.

First curve unit on top of the next fabric to determine the next curved cut

Trim Ears and Tails and Line Up New Fabrics with the Pizza Shape

Use a ruler to trim off the ears and tails as you go and line up the new fabric with the pizza shape before you cut. Your blocks will be more likely to end up close to the same size.

8. Put the new pizza shape from the third fabric aside for later. Cut a new curve from the larger crust piece, either wider or narrower than the first one. The new curve can also be wider at one end and narrower at the other.

9. Sew the new curve to the Step 6 unit. Press towards the pizza.

10. Choose a fourth fabric for your next curve and layer it underneath the block in progress *right sides up*. Cut the new fabric along the outer curve you just sewed.

11. Put aside the pizza piece from the fourth fabric. Cut a new curve from the larger crust piece varying the size and shape, then sew it to the Step 9 unit as before.

Four curves in different colors

12. Continue adding new fabrics and cutting new curves until your block is the size you want. Aim for 5–7 colors in a variety of values and curve shapes. Trim the edges to get the largest block you can.

Basic curve block

Consider cutting a new pizza piece in an opposite corner from your first one. This is a good way to make the block have more energy. The new pizza shape can be just one element or several, but it's a good idea to make it smaller or simpler than the first corner.

Your pizza elements don't have to be plain. Using an Angled Stripe unit (page 43) for an initial pizza curve or an opposite pizza curve can add interesting lines and shapes to your composition. I suggest that you use this kind of element more than once in a design so it doesn't seem random.

Any Which Way using Angled Stripe elements

skinny lines

Skinny lines create interest because they are such a change from the usual width of your curves, especially if you use a highly contrasting color or value. Sometimes I use a print fabric for my skinny lines for an unexpected pop. They are best used in moderation to help draw the eye around the composition.

Supernova by Cindy Grisdela, 40″ × 54″, 2023

Supernova (above) is a good example of using skinny lines to draw the eye. I used narrow yellow/gold lines both in the blocks and cutting through some of the blocks to create striking diagonal lines.

1. Cut skinny lines about ¾″ wide for any of the curves after the first pizza cut.

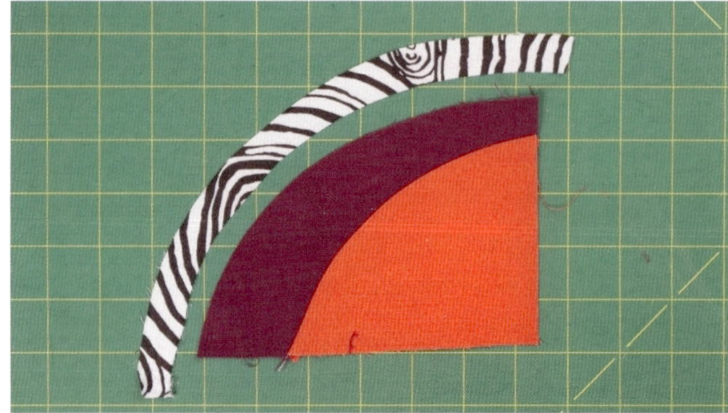

Skinny line cut ¾″ wide

2. Sew the skinny line curve to the existing unit.

3. With right sides together, pin the next curve to the skinny line piece. For just this seam, pin with the pizza unit on top so you can see the first seam line. To make the skinny line more even and less organic, sew the second curve of the skinny line piece from the skinny line side, aligning the presser foot with the seam sewn in Step 2 instead of lining up the raw edges as you usually do. If needed, after sewing trim the seam allowance to ¼″.

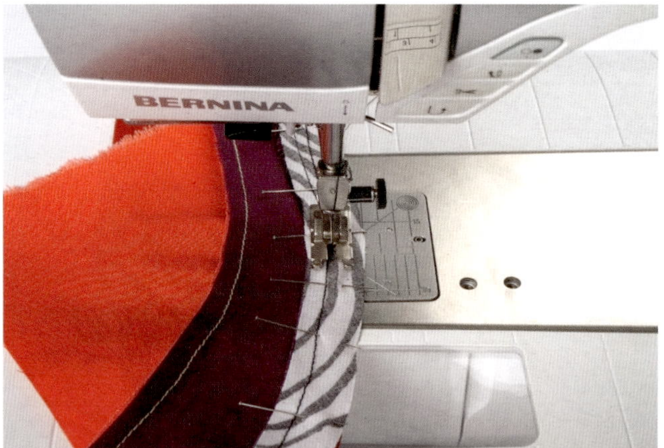

Sewing the second skinny line seam with the presser foot lined up with the left seam.

Using this method, you can get a line as narrow as ⅛″ and it will look more regular on the front, avoiding wobbling that can occur if your cut line isn't completely even with the edge, which it often isn't with freehand cutting.

Practice Curves
Presser feet vary among machines. Try some practice curves to see where you need to position the presser foot in relation to the previously sewn seam to get the width you want. Remember, you are aligning this new seam with the previous seam rather than the raw edge!

4. Press the second seam away from the pizza shape and trim the seam allowance to ¼″ if needed. Always press seams away from the skinny line to reduce bulk in the block. Trim the edges to get the largest block you can.

Skinny line block

Back of skinny line block with seams pressed away

belly curves

Belly Curves add a new line and shape to your block that can be unexpected. It's natural to cut your curves in a similar way once you find a comfortable rhythm. This is a good way to shake things up a little bit. I'm always looking for ways to keep my blocks from looking too predictable.

1. Layer a unit containing several elements on top of another fabric square *right sides up*. Cut the crust fabric along the outer edge of the sewn unit.

2. Put the pizza shape from the new fabric aside and cut a curve from the new fabric that "bellies" out in the center with narrower curves on the top and bottom.

Belly curve cut

3. Pin from the center out and sew the seam as before.

4. Continue adding elements until the block is the size you want. Trim the edges to get the largest block you can.

Belly curve block

fried egg curves

Fried Egg Curves are a similar way to add an unexpected line and shape to your block. I use this technique in the middle of a block to give plenty of room for the wavy curve. It's less effective in the smaller corners.

1. Layer a unit in process on top of another square *right sides up*. Cut the new fabric along the outer edge of the sewn unit to establish the seam line.

2. Put the new pizza shape aside for later and cut a wavy "fried egg" type line from the new crust fabric instead of cutting a straight curve. Try to keep the curves gentle and not too steep.

Fried egg curve cut

3. Pin from the center out and sew the seam as before, stopping when needed to realign the raw edges. The curves will look like they won't fit together when you put them right sides together, but they will fit because you cut the curves at the same time. Because the curve changes direction from concave to convex, you'll need to be extra careful to keep the raw edges aligned as you sew. I sew the seam from one side to the other, but you may consider sewing from the center to one side, then turning the unit upside down and sewing from the center to the other side to help keep the curves aligned.

4. Continue adding elements until the block is the size you want. Trim the edges to get the largest block you can.

Fried egg block

Wavy Seams

Sometimes it's difficult to get the fried egg seams to lie flat. Using steam when pressing and clipping the curves may help. If it's really wonky, try using your iron to press the seam where it wants to go to lie flat. Then resew that portion of the seam using the ironed line as a guide. Trim the seam to ¼″. This tip can help tame any seams that don't want to lie flat, not just the fried egg seams.

Wavy curve won't lie flat

After pressing

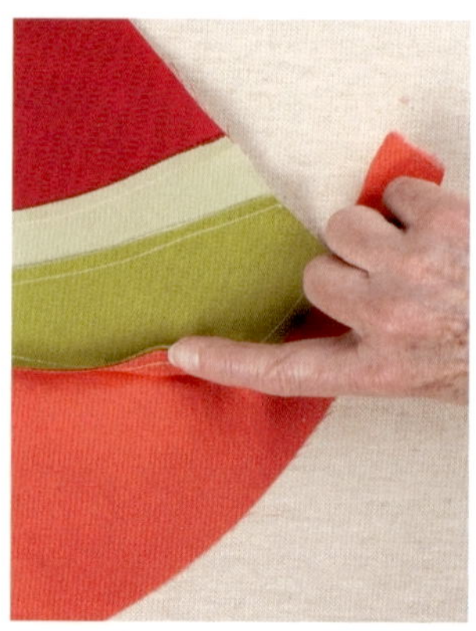

Press the curve flat and restitch on the pressed line.

insets

Insets—strips of fabric inserted into larger pieces in a block—can break up the lines in the block in a variety of ways. Narrow insets can go either in the curved elements or in the pizza shape. They can be plain, pieced, or prints. Wider insets in the curve create an interesting optical illusion where they can blend into the background or other strips. Pieced units in a larger curve add a pop of contrast that creates dimension and texture.

1. To add insets to a curved element, cut the curve between 2″ and 3″ wide. The insets will take up some of the seam allowance, so I usually cut and sew the inset curve before deciding what elements will go on either side of it.

Insets can be any size and any number. Mine are usually cut about 1″ wide to finish at ½″ because I like the narrow look. You can make them the same color or different colors.

2. Lay the insets on your curve where you want them to go.

3. Cut the background curve on *one side* of each inset to create a place to sew the inset into the background.

Insets laid on background curve

4. Sew the insets into the curve right sides together. Press away from the inset.

5. Sometimes the edges are a little ragged after inserting the insets. If needed, recut the curve using the prior unit as a guide to clean up the edge.

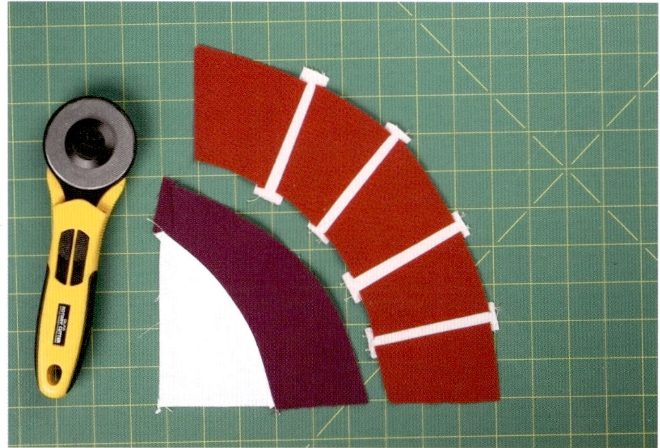

Use the prior unit to recut a ragged curve with a rotary cutter.

6. Sew the inset curve to the prior unit as normal and continue adding curves until your block is the size you want. Trim the edges to get the largest block you can.

Inset Curve block

VARIATIONS ON INSETS

Consider variations on the inset. Wider insets using the same or similar fabrics as one of the curves touching them can be interesting because of the optical illusion created—does the eye see the inset or the background?

Wide pink insets with pink elements above and below create an optical illusion in *Any Which Way*.

Use some of the scraps from trimming your blocks to make scrappy insets. These are most effective if the curve is wider to show off the tiny compositions.

Inset block with scrappy insets

Consider adding insets to your pizza shapes, either plain lines or stripes. Place the inset on the pizza shape where you want it to go, then cut an opening in the pizza on one side of the inset.

Pieced inset in pizza

Sew the inset into the pizza shape, right sides together. If needed, trim the curve to eliminate any ragged edge.

Any Which Way detail with pieced inset

wonky triangle curves

Wonky triangles are a fun way to add new lines and shapes to your blocks. I construct them either two at a time or using a scrappy approach.

TWO AT A TIME WONKY TRIANGLE CURVES

1. Stack 2 squares 15″ × 15″ or use leftover squares with a pizza shape cut out of them, right sides up. They should be either different colors or different values of the same color so that there is a contrast between them. Cut a graceful curve about 3″ tall through both layers.

Initial curves for wonky triangles

2. Cut rough triangle shapes through both layers. They don't have to be the same size or shape. Leave at least 1″ separation between the lower edges of the triangles so there's room for seam allowances.

3. Shuffle the shapes so there are 2 curves with different color triangles and backgrounds.

Shuffled triangle curves

4. Carefully lay out the shuffled triangle curves next to your sewing machine and sew the triangles onto the backgrounds to complete the curved shape.

5. Use the curves in 2 different blocks. If needed, recut the curve using the pizza unit you want this curve to join with as a guide to remove any ragged edges and sew the triangle curve onto your block.

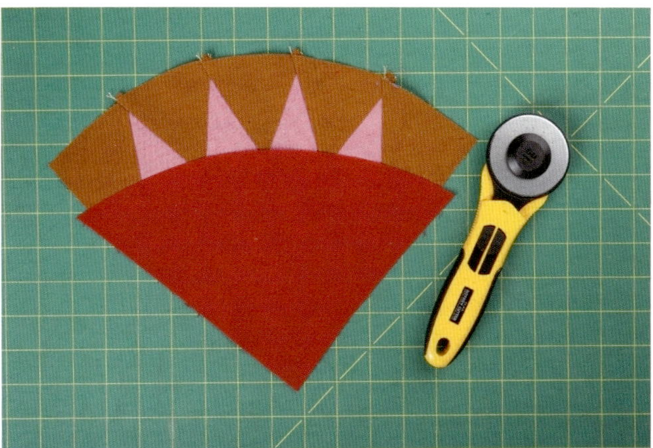

Trim ragged edge of triangle curve

Wonky Triangle block

BELLY CURVE TRIANGLES

1. To make a Wonky Triangle Curve with a slightly different look, cut your initial curves with a belly. The new shape makes it easy to cut triangles of different sizes.

2. Shuffle the triangles so there are 2 curves.

Belly cut triangle curves

3. Sew the triangles together as before and use the resulting curves in 2 different blocks.

Curves Around detail with belly cut triangle

Triangle Points
If you want the triangles in the curve to end in a defined point, make sure to cut the triangles to come to a point at the top instead of a blunt edge. These shapes are Improv, so they won't be as crisp as they would be if they were paper pieced, but cutting to a point at the top will help.

SCRAPPY TRIANGLE CURVE

Sometimes you just want one triangle curve, and you have scraps left over from your blocks or from another project. Or maybe you want to make your triangles even more wonky.

Fiesta detail with scrappy triangle curve

1. Choose a background fabric and cut a 3″-wide curve. It can be a new 15″ × 15″ square or a leftover piece from another block. Just make sure it's long enough to hold at least 3 triangle shapes.

2. From your scraps, rough cut a few triangles. Vary their height and angle if you want to. The triangles can be the same color or different colors.

3. Lay the cut triangles on top of the background curve. Remember to leave at least 1″ between the bottom of each triangle so the seam allowances don't overlap once sewn.

Scrappy triangles on background

4. Carefully cut the background on each side of your triangle. Remove the bonus triangles underneath and sew the scrappy triangles into the background.

Scrappy Triangles cut with bonus triangles

Your curve will be smaller than you cut it initially because of the seam allowances, so I often wait until the curve is sewn before deciding what pizza shape to add to it. This is a good time to use pizza shapes left over from previous blocks.

Scrappy triangle curve

5. Continue to build your block until it is the size you want. Trim the edges to get the largest block you can.

confetti pops

Confetti pops are a great way to add repetition and movement to your blocks. They can be either wonky and offset in the curve, or more evenly spaced. Or maybe you can think of another way to design them. Use your creativity!

Supernova by Cindy Grisdela, 40″ × 54″, 2023

OFFSET POPS IN THE CURVE

1. Start with a 15″ × 15″ square. This will be your background.

2. Cut a generous size pizza shape from 1 corner of the block. Put it aside for later use. Or, use a leftover shape from a previous block that already has a pizza cut out of it.

3. Cut squares or rectangles for your pops in a variety of colors—about 1½″ × 1½″ or 1½″ × 2″. They don't have to be cut exactly with a ruler or all be the same size, but they should contrast in color, value, or both, with the background fabric.

4. Arrange the pops in a pleasing manner in your design on top of the background you're using. Leave at least 1″–1½″ between each pop. Sometimes I use 1 fewer pop than I think I want just so they don't look crowded after sewing. A good rule of thumb is 5 pops for a 15″ square.

Confetti pops laid on background

5. Using a ruler, cut along each side of your pops with a straight vertical cut. Next make a horizontal cut through the background at the *top* of each pop to divide the background into an upper and a lower stem relative to the pop. *Do not cut the pop!*

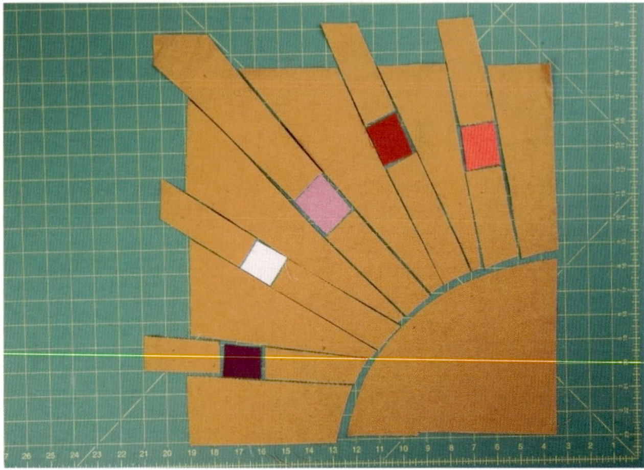

Cut lines to create stems

6. Sew the stems onto the bottom and top of the pops. Press toward the pop.

7. The pop and stem will form a straight line, while the background pieces will be wedge shaped. Arrange the pop units in a fan radiating out from the pizza. Align the bottom edges of the pop stems and the background wedges as much as possible.

8. Starting in the center, sew the pops and the background wedges together, right sides together. Press away from the pop stems.

Confetti Pop Units are Smaller
Sewing the pops into the background in a staggered placement results in a much smaller finished element because of the seam allowances that are taken up. I usually make the confetti pop unit first before deciding how to add the other elements to the block. If it's still too small, consider recutting the edge pieces to make them larger or simply adding another piece of the same fabric to the edges that are too short. The seam won't show once it's quilted.

Sewn pop wedge

9. Measure the size of the confetti pop unit. Ideally it will be at least 12″ × 12″. If it isn't, you can add a coping element to make it bigger. See Puzzling Blocks Together, page 38.

10. Choose a pizza unit to sew onto the open corner of the wedge. It can be a single shape or a combination of different elements.

11. Recut the confetti pop curve using the pizza unit as a guide and sew the pop section to the pizza shape, pinning from the center out.

12. Either leave the opposite corner as is or consider adding another pizza unit to the opposite corner to complete your block.

Confetti pop block

Adding an Element to a Finished Block

If you decide to add an element to a finished block that has already been trimmed to size, lay the new element on the finished block offset by about ½″ before cutting. The overlap will account for the seam allowance and help your block to remain the same size it was before you added the new piece.

Add opposite pizza to already trimmed block

Supernova detail with offset confetti pops

CONFETTI POPS–STRAIGHT CURVE

Confetti pops that are offset in the curve add energy and variety to your composition. Confetti pops set in a straight curve add motion and repetition in a more ordered way. Sometimes I use both types in a design and sometimes just one or the other. In *Twist and Shout* (below), I used both types to move the eye around my composition, and *Fiesta* (page 9) just has the offset type.

Twist and Shout by Cindy Grisdela, 46″x 48″, 2022

Two types of confetti pop blocks

1. Choose a 15″ × 15″ square background fabric and cut a pizza shape out of 1 corner. If you have a piece of fabric with a "bite" taken out of one corner it's fine to use that, because you will create a different pizza unit to add in its place. I usually wait to decide what exactly the corner element will contain until I've made the confetti pops.

2. Rough cut squares or rectangles from your scraps for the pops, about 1½″ × 1½″ or 1½″ × 2″. They don't need to be precise. This is a good time to add pops of brighter or darker colors than you have in the rest of your design.

3. Lay the squares on top of the background fabric in a graceful curve from the center of the pizza corner to the opposite corner. Leave about 1″ between each pop and don't put them too close to either edge on the top and bottom.

4. Cut a 1½″-wide strip from the leftover background piece.

Pops on background with 1½″ strip

5. Cut the background strip into sections to go between the pops. It's ok to just eyeball it.

To preserve the curve while sewing, cut slight angles in the background shapes to make wedges that go between the pops. The pop should remain square or rectangular. Don't make the wedge too steep and make sure the wide ends are all at the top of the curve and the narrow ends at the bottom. If you reverse them, the curve will serpentine, which might be something else to try!

Pops with background wedges

6. Sew the pops to the background wedges. Press towards the pops.

7. Lay the curve on top of the background pieces right sides up. Cut the background along the top of the curve to make the curves match and clean up any ragged edges on the pop curve.

8. Press away from the pop curve. Lay the sewn element on top of the other half of the background, lining up the corner edges. Recut if necessary to make the curves match and clean up any ragged edges on the pop curve.

9. Sew the second curve to the first unit.

angel wings

There is still space in the curved block to add something more. You could add another pop curve or two, or a couple of plain curved lines. Often, I combine the curved pop with Angel Wing curves. I discovered these by accident one day when I was making blocks and playing with leftovers, which is one of the reasons why I put my leftover pieces aside and go through them as I work. You never know what good ideas are in there!

The Angel Wing is simply a gentle curve that is wider at the bottom and narrower at the top. I like to add them on either side of the curved pop going in opposite directions to reinforce the curved line and add a new color and shape. Decide if you want the Angel Wings to be the same color or two different colors. Look at the colors and values you have in your blocks so far. Are there any that seem to need a friend? Sometimes darker or lighter values stand out in the design and if you add the same or similar value in another place, it helps to even out the visual texture.

Supernova detail with Pops and Angel Wings

1. Decide on the color or colors to accent the pop curve unit and cut 2 Angel Wing curves from scraps or leftover fabric.

2. Lay the curves right sides up on top of the completed unit to decide on placement.

Angel Wings on background

3. Cut the background fabric along the edge of 1 of the curves so the curves will match up when sewn.

4. Sew the Angel Wing curve into the background.

5. Lay the unit back on top of the background piece that was left when you made the first cut and line up the edges in the corner sections. Cut the second curve of the Angel Wing unit and sew.

6. Repeat for the Angel Wing on the other side of the pop unit.

Sewn Angel Wings and Pops

7. Decide on the pizza shape to add to the curved pop and Angel Wing unit. It can be 1 element or a combination.

8. Lay the pizza shape on top of the Angel Wing unit right sides up and cut the unit along the pizza shape to make the curves match and get rid of the ragged edges.

9. Sew the pizza shape into the Angel Wing unit.

These blocks are usually a dramatic element that draws the eye into the design, so I often put them on an outside corner. Consider making a double block for even more drama. The lower right corner of *Twist and Shout* (page 11) is a 12″ × 24″ unit with a sweeping curve pop and Angel Wings. Note the lighter purple skinny curve between the pop curve and the lower Angel Wing. It's subtle but adds something unexpected to the block.

Twist and Shout detail with Angel Wings and Pops in a 12″ × 24″ double block

puzzling blocks together

After you've completed a collection of blocks using the techniques in the last chapter, it's time to figure out how to put them together into a quilt. If you trimmed your blocks to the largest square or rectangle you could get out of each one, you will likely have blocks in a variety of sizes. Now the fun begins!

Start by putting your blocks up on the design wall or other surface, if you haven't already. Don't worry at this point about whether anything fits or how you will sew it together. Just look for connections between the blocks in color, line, and shape.

Twist and Shout (page 11) is an exploration of a variety of gray values that contrast with bright colors. I had intended to make a neutral quilt, but a few brights snuck in and then a few more, and before I knew it, the design had morphed into an entirely new idea. It's one of the reasons I am drawn to Improv design—each decision about color and shape influences the next, so the original idea changes as the design emerges on the wall.

Twist and Shout by Cindy Grisdela, 46″ × 48″, 2022

Often the tendency is to put four blocks together to make a circle, and sometimes that's the right choice. If you do opt for the circle idea, some of the blocks will have more curves or other elements in one corner, while the opposite corner is simpler. I call the dense corner the drama corner. Consider creating your circle with the drama corner of two or three blocks in the center and one or two blocks with the less complicated element contrasting with them.

Twist and Shout detail with center curve

In the center of *Twist and Shout* (page 11), I used three blocks with a lot of energy in the upper left, lower left, and lower right, along with a fourth block in the upper right that is just one pizza shape with an inset. The contrast creates visual texture that makes the circle more appealing than it might otherwise be.

The opposite pizza element with more curves can relate to another block and start a new conversation.

Another point about this detail is the way the grays "break the block" and create a new shape. Often in more traditional quiltmaking, we avoid having blocks containing the same or similar colors touch each other, because that blurs the block shape. But in Improv quilting, it can be a design feature to allow colors to create new shapes, regardless of the block seam lines.

I used mostly blue grays in this design, but there is one mushroom gray in the mix that is more brown than the rest. On the left side of this detail, the mushroom gray in the top block with the confetti pops connects to the one below it with multicolor insets, obscuring the seam line of the block and creating a new shape. The blue grays on the right side of the block do the same thing.

In *Any Which Way* (below), I used this idea to intentionally construct a large shape in the right center of the quilt. The charcoal dog bone in the right middle block draws the eye into the design and meets the pizza shape of a similar color in the center block. The center bottom block has a narrow charcoal curve that connects with a wider charcoal curve in the lower right block, which merges with the dog bone above to visually complete the shape.

Any Which Way by Cindy Grisdela, 38″x 39″, 2024

Look for areas where the colors form new shapes.

In the upper left section of the quilt, I used dark pink and orange to draw the eye into a serpentine shape from the upper left corner through the orange fried egg curve in the center block through the pizza shape above it in the top center and the wonky triangles in the top right.

These connections are possible because I designed the blocks on the wall so I could see how the colors and shapes related to each other as I worked. As you design, look for opportunities to "break the block" and use color to draw new shapes and move the eye around your composition.

Remember to take photos as the design takes shape, in case you decide that an earlier placement of your elements is the best one.

There are other options. In *'70s Serpentine* (below) there are no circles at all, and each block relates to the others to form a serpentine or cog shape.

'70s Serpentine, by Cindy Grisdela 54″ × 54″, 2025

Fiesta has two diagonal circles in the design moving from upper left to lower right.

Fiesta by Cindy Grisdela, 32″ × 33″, 2022

Twist and Shout (page 11) has a combination of full circles and partial circles, plus a serpentine element in the upper right.

There are no rules in this process, so you get to decide what colors to use, what elements you want to include, and how improvisational you want your blocks to be. You don't have to use all the elements and techniques I've discussed in each quilt! Choose the ones that resonate with you the most or that you enjoy making and go from there. If your blocks are not quite coming together for you, see Design Tricks (page 48).

coping elements

Once you are satisfied with the arrangement of your blocks, it's time to figure out how to sew them together. There are several ways to add elements to your composition to fill in the gaps. I call these coping strips, because they are necessary to "cope" with the blocks being different sizes.

Why not just trim the blocks to be all the same size, you might ask?

That's certainly an option, but I think there are times when the need to create bridges between the blocks makes for a more compelling design.

Demo blocks to puzzle together

Photo by Cindy Grisdela

I laid out the demo blocks I made for the Techniques chapter (page 20) to find a pleasing arrangement. There are three gaps where the blocks need coping elements—above the center block, between the lower right block with the confetti pops and the bottom middle block with the inset compositions, and between the bottom right confetti pop block and the block above it.

The easiest one to deal with is the last one—the space between the bottom right confetti pop block and the one above it. The confetti pop block is smaller than the rest, so I added a purple strip to the top of the block that is a similar value to the purple in the block above. The seam won't show when it's quilted.

Adding a filler strip of fabric in the same or similar color is a good way to visually extend a block shape.

For the other two gaps, I added checkerboard row strips—one of my favorite coping elements when the space to fill is no more than about 2″.

CHECKERBOARD ROW STRIPS

1. Determine the finished width of the space to be filled with a checkerboard row and add ½″ to find the cut width for each strip.

2. Choose one of the lightest values and one of the darkest values in the design for your checkerboard row.

3. Cut a strip from each fabric the width calculated in Step 1 and sew them together along one of the long sides.

4. Press the seam to the darker fabric. Cut sections from the strip equal to the Step 1 measurement.

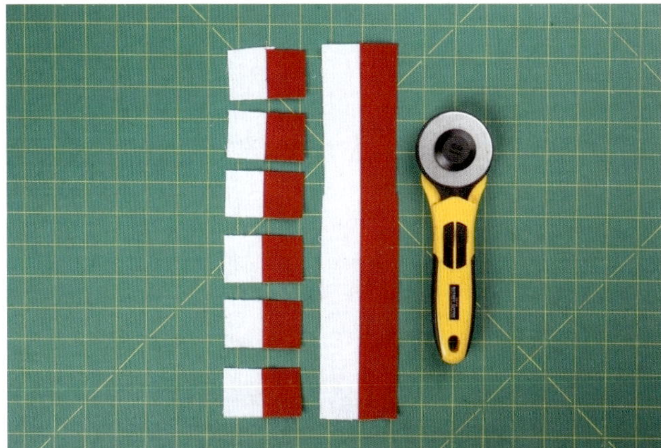

Checkerboard row strip set and cutting sections

5. Lay the sections on your design gap. Consider replacing one or more of the dark values with a bright pop.

6. Sew the sections together to complete the checkerboard row strip.

Checkerboard row with bright pop replacements

Demo quilt with coping elements

Photo by Cindy Grisdela

Fiesta by Cindy Grisdela, 32″ × 33″, 2022

In *Fiesta* (left), one of my first freehand curve quilts, I used a vertical checkerboard row strip between two blocks on the upper left to address the fact that the upper left block was smaller than the one next to it. And I added a longer horizontal checkerboard row strip in the lower right section to make that section the same size as the two blocks on the lower left.

It's more interesting if you have the strips going both vertically and horizontally in the design, rather than two strips going the same direction. So, I pay attention to that as I'm working and sometimes will add another checkerboard row strip even if I don't technically need it to balance the flow.

Consider Prints

If you are short on time, commercial stripes or checkerboards work well as coping strips if you have a commercial print that complements your composition.

Twist and Shout detail with print coping strip

ANGLED STRIPES

If there are larger gaps to fill, Angled Stripe units might be the answer. First a little background.

Blue Eyes by Cindy Grisdela, 52″ × 53″, 2022

I set a few guidelines for the design of *Blue Eyes* (above). The color palette would be values of blue, from light cornflower to turquoise to lake blue to navy. The elements used would be basic curves, fried egg and belly curves, insets, and wonky triangles. The triangles and insets would be black and white, except for the pieced insets in some of the pizza shapes.

As I started creating blocks, it became apparent that using the spiky wonky triangle units added a lot of energy to the piece and it quickly became too busy.

That's another one of the things I enjoy about the Improv process—the ability to revise as the piece takes shape on the wall. Time for some new guidelines.

Angled Stripes are one of my favorite Improv units, as you know if you've read my other books. They are versatile and easy to piece, and they add interest in all kinds of ways—as complete blocks or cut up into narrower stripes.

Choose Your Size

As a rule of thumb, cut the fabrics for Angled Stripes blocks into rectangles that are ½″–1″ taller and 2″–2½″ wider than you want the sewn block to be. A 7″ × 9″ stack of rectangles will make 6½″ finished blocks, which is a good size for many designs. If you just want stripes, cut the rectangles ½″–1″ taller than you want the stripe to be and any width. For example, a 4″ × 9″ stack of rectangles will give you 3½″ × 7″ stripes or two sets of 1½″ × 7″ stripes.

1. Choose 5–8 fabrics that complement your blocks in a variety of colors and values. For *Blue Eyes* I chose a medium royal blue, navy, 2 values of turquoise, 2 values of gray, and 2 light blue values.

2. Cut the fabrics into rectangles. See Choose Your Size (above) for suggested sizes. I needed 10½″ × 10½″ squares for *Blue Eyes*, so I cut my rectangles 11″ × 13″.

Cut rectangles for Angled Stripes

3. Arrange the rectangles in a pleasing order, varying the colors and values. If your fabrics have a right and a wrong side, arrange them for cutting *right sides up*.

4. Make angled cuts through all layers. Vary the slant and width of each cut for more interest. The number of cuts to make depends on the number of fabrics you started with. If you have 7 fabrics, make 6 cuts—1 cut fewer than the number of fabrics.

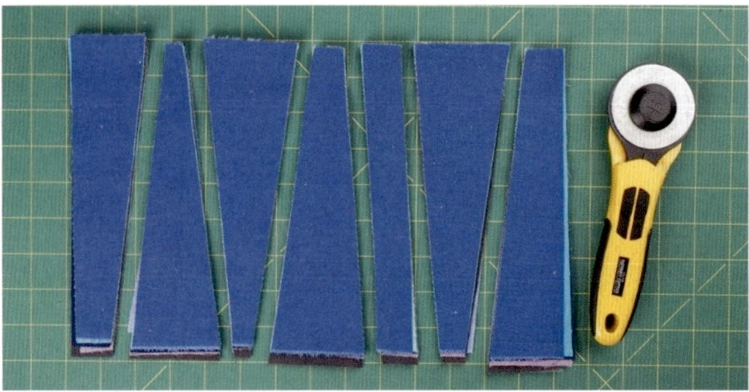

Angled cuts

5. Leave the leftmost stack as is. Shuffle the stacks to make the stripes.

6. For the second stack, move the top fabric to the bottom. On the third stack, move the top 2 fabrics to the bottom. Continue with each stack, moving 1 more piece to the bottom until you have shuffled the whole set and there is a different fabric on top of each stack.

Shuffled cuts

Mark the Left Edge

Put a straight pin through the top left corner of each fabric in the leftmost stack to remind you that is the edge of the Angled Stripes block, and you won't be sewing anything to that side.

7. Sew the blocks together. They can be sewn individually by taking the top fabric from each stack and laying it down beside your sewing machine. See Chain Piecing (below) for a fast way to chain piece the units.

8. Press the seams to one side and trim the blocks to the desired size.

Don't Worry if They Get Mixed Up
If your stacks get mixed up and you have the same fabric twice in one block, it's okay! These blocks provide visual texture to the design without being too busy. No one will stop to count to make sure that each block has all different fabrics in it.

Angled stripes blocks

CHAIN PIECING THE BLOCKS

Chain piecing is a fast way to sew blocks together that helps to keep the fabrics in order and reduces the chance of mixing up the stacks as you sew.

1. To sew, start with the 2 leftmost stacks. Take the top fabric from each stack and piece them right sides together using a ¼″ seam, creating a unit of 2 stripes each. Repeat with the next pair of top fabrics. Don't cut the threads between each pair.

2. When all the pairs from those stacks are sewn, stop and reach behind the sewing machine to bring the first pair forward. Cut the thread connecting *just that 1 pair* from its neighbor and pick up the top fabric from the third stack.

Chain pieced pairs at the sewing machine

3. Sew the third fabric to the pair you just cut off from the chain, making sure to attach it to the side of the pair without the pin. Don't cut the thread.

4. Reach back and bring the next pair forward. Clip the thread connecting just that pair from its neighbor and add the next fabric from the third stack to that pair.

5. Keep sewing until all fabrics have been added to the first pairs and you have 3 fabrics in each unit. You will have a continuous chain of units.

6. Repeat the process until all the blocks have been sewn, cutting only 1 unit from the chain at a time.

7. Cut the blocks apart and press the seams to one side.

In *Blue Eyes* (page 43) I used the Angled Stripes blocks to add space and texture between the curved blocks. One benefit of these blocks was being able to dramatically offset the curved blocks, so the centers didn't match at all.

In some areas I cut the striped blocks into narrow strips to fill in odd spaces. This is an option for coping strips even if you aren't using the blocks themselves. See Choose Your Size (page 44) for suggested sizes for the rectangles if you only want narrow stripes instead of full blocks.

Blue Eyes detail with mismatched curve centers

LOG CABIN POPS

Often as my quilts unfold, there are still gaps left to be filled. They seem too large for checkerboard rows and I want something other than stripes.

Log Cabin pops are another coping element that works to fill in open areas in the design. I make them from two different fabrics—a center pop and a background—because I want the pops to stand out. The seams in the background don't show once it's quilted and it looks like the pops are floating.

For *Blue Eyes* I made the pops 3½″ × 3½″ to finish at 3″ × 3″ when sewn in.

1. Choose 2 contrasting fabrics from the palette you are using. Decide which will be the pop and which the background. Consider making the pop a slightly different color or value than your other fabrics. The pops in *Blue Eyes* are red purple, which adds a bit of contrast to the blues.

2. For a 3½″ × 3½″ pop block, cut a 1½″ × 1½″ square from your contrasting fabric.

3. Cut a 1½″-wide strip from the background fabric, then subcut the strip into a 1½″ × 1½″ square, 2 rectangles 1½″ × 2½″, and 1 rectangle 1½″ × 3½″. If you don't want to use precise measurements, you can just cut the shapes without a ruler and square it up later.

Blue Eyes detail with pops

Deconstructed Log Cabin pop

4. Sew the center pop and the 1½″ × 1½″ background square together first, then add the other rectangles to the center unit in a counter clockwise manner, ending with the 1½″ × 3½″ strip.

5. The finished pop should measure about 3½″ × 3½″ square.

6. Make as many pops as needed to fill the gap. If needed, trim the blocks slightly to fit when sewing.

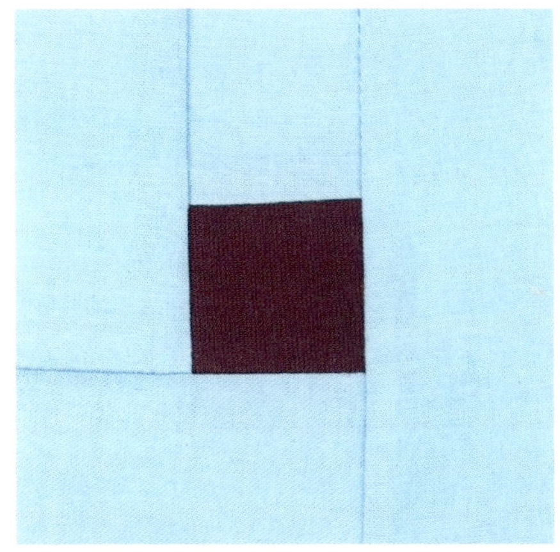

Log Cabin pop

POPS ANOTHER WAY

If you need your pops to be smaller and closer together to fill the gap, use this method.

1. Cut the desired number of pops from your contrast fabric in the size you want, 1½″ × 1½″ for example.

2. Cut 2 background squares 1½″ × 1½″ for each pop.

3. Cut a 1½″-wide strip from the background fabric. Subcut the strip into 1½″ × 3½″ rectangles. Cut 1 more rectangle than you have pops. For 3 pops you need 4 rectangles, for example.

4. Sew the 2 background squares onto the top and bottom of a pop square. Press toward the pop.

5. Repeat for all of the contrast pops.

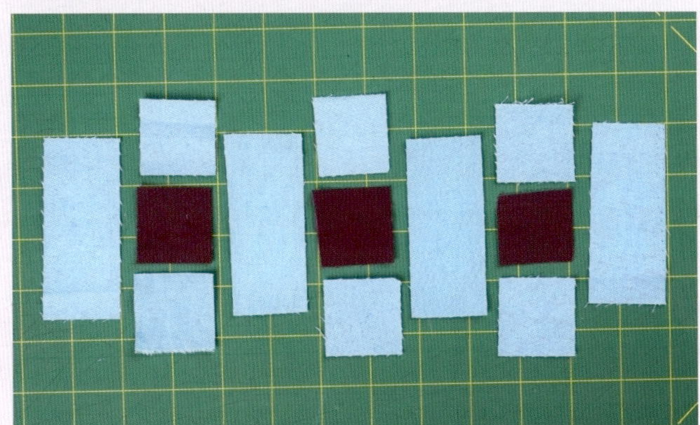

Deconstructed pops version 2

6. Alternate the Step 4 pops and the background rectangles, with 1 background piece on each end of the row. Sew the unit together.

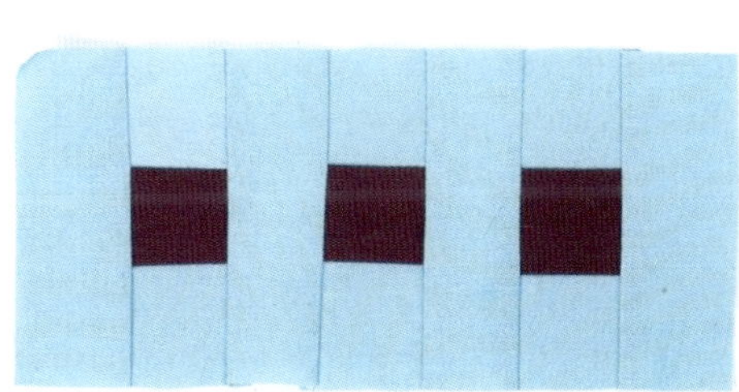

Completed pops version 2

To make even smaller pops, about 2½″ tall:

1. Cut the pops and the 2 background 1″ × 1″ squares. Sew the sets together.

2. Cut the background strips 1″ × 2½″ and alternate them with the pop sets.

3. Sew the unit together as above.

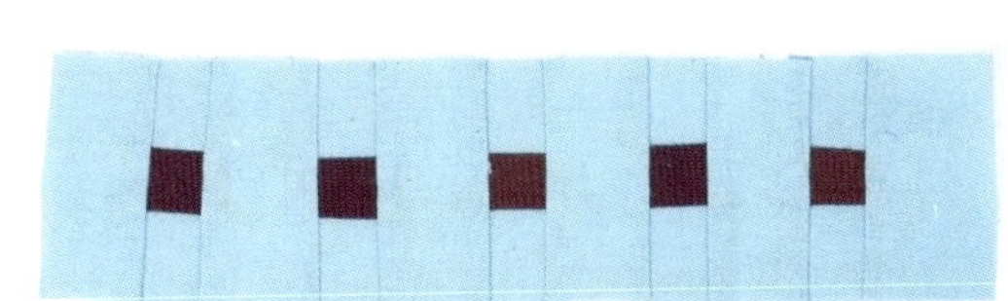

Tiny pop unit

design tricks

What if your design needs more than just arranging the blocks in a different way or adding a checkerboard row stripe to fill in a gap? That happens to everyone at one time or another. It's one of the joys and one of the challenges of designing improvisationally without a pattern.

If the initial composition you put up on the design wall from the blocks you made in the techniques chapter isn't coming together the way you hoped, there are a variety of strategies to consider to make things better, from adding a few simple blocks to the design to cutting into some of the blocks to add a pop of contrast.

SIMPLE BLOCKS

Sometimes the design is too busy and there's no place for the eye to rest. This happened during the construction of *Blue Eyes* (page 43). The energy of the black and white wonky triangles overwhelmed everything else. The solution was adding in four simple blocks to calm the composition. Each one had one pizza shape in blue or teal with a black and white pieced inset on a turquoise crust block.

These blocks act to provide negative space in different areas of the quilt that gives the eye a place to rest. You can see them in the second block from the left on the top row, the second block up from the bottom left, in the center right middle, and the lower right.

Blue Eyes detail simple block

COPING CURVES

Sometimes despite your best efforts, some of the blocks just aren't very interesting. One way to deal with that outcome is to add coping curves.

In *Supernova* (page 31), there were several blocks that needed some help. The second block down from the top on the left and the second block down from the top on the right both seemed plainer than I liked. To add energy and a pop of contrast, I cut a narrow gold curve from scrap fabric and inserted it into the middle of the block.

The gold curves complemented the skinny gold lines elsewhere in the design and helped to move the eye around the composition, drawing attention away from the blocks that seemed too ordinary.

1. Choose a block that could be more striking.

2. Cut a narrow curve in a contrasting color or value to insert into the block.

3. Lay the curve on the block where you think it will be most effective.

Block with curve laid in

4. Carefully cut the block using the top of the curve as a guide. Sew the first side of the curve into the block. Press away from the curve.

5. Sew the second side of the curve into the block using the Skinny Line technique (page 24). Press away from the curve.

6. Consider adding another curve going in the opposite direction and remember that the block will end up smaller than it was because of the seam allowances.

Finished Coping Curve block

Supernova by Cindy Grisdela, 40″ × 54″, 2023

Coping curves through the whole block

putting it all together

Once you have added in the coping elements you need to fill in any gaps in your composition and you are happy with your layout, it's time to sew it all together.

If your blocks are offset in the design, it helps to take a photo to help you see where the seam lines are. Use a contrasting pen or marker to draw the seam lines right on the photo for reference at the sewing machine.

Seams Don't Need to Match

The seams of your blocks don't have to match up in this process. As long as you are able to create units that can be sewn together, the offset seams don't matter, and they often add a pleasing twist to the composition.

Baby Blues by Cindy Grisdela, 20″ × 20″, 2024

Baby Blues (above) is a simple four block design. The blocks vary widely in size and the center is wildly offset, adding to its charm. This design was made with left over elements from *Blue Eyes* (page 43). See Using Leftovers (page 57).

Blue Eyes with seam lines drawn

Blue Eyes (page 43) was relatively easy to construct once the coping elements were included, even though the blocks are different sizes and the block centers don't match. There are four large quadrants of varying sizes.

The four blocks in the lower left quadrant are the same height when they are sewn into two pairs, so they fit together. The six blocks in the upper left are sewn into three pairs of two blocks that are the same height.

On the right side of the quilt, nine blocks in the upper right section go together into a rough nine-patch. The three blocks at the bottom of the nine-patch are the same height, so they can be sewn together into a row. The top block on the upper right and the one below it are the same width, so they can be sewn together. The remaining four blocks to the left are the same height, so they can be sewn together into two rows, making a rough four-patch.

I sewed the four-patch blocks to the vertical block section, then that unit to the three-block row to create that unit.

In the lower right, the six blocks are sewn into pairs that are either the same width or the same height, then combined into a larger unit.

Once those four units are constructed, the composition can be completed by sewing the quadrants together.

I paid no attention to the centers of the blocks, just put them together into units that were the same height or the same width. I like the visual texture the mismatch creates in the composition.

Supernova (page 14) was more complex to put together, although the coping strips were simpler. I deliberately made each of the ten blocks in the composition a different size as a challenge to see how they would fit together. The taller block on the lower left complements the tall block on the upper right with curved pops drawing the eye into the design.

Supernova deconstructed

There is a plain black coping strip in the upper left quadrant to make the two blocks on the right of that section the same height as the blocks on the left. The black strip blends into the black pizza shape in the bottom block, which blurs the seam line and implies a new shape. Those four blocks can then be sewn together as a unit.

The three blocks in the lower left go together as a unit without any coping elements, but it's a couple of inches wider than the unit above.

The two stacked blocks on the lower right are narrower than the upper right block, which needed a black coping strip at the top to make it the right height. That leaves a rectangular gap just to the left of the quilt center.

This gap will have to be filled with partial seaming. A partial seam is a method for inserting a shape into the design at a right angle. To begin, measure the gap to be filled, including seam allowances, and cut the coping element to fit. You will sew part of the first seam, backstitch, and leave the unsewn edge open. Then sew the remaining three complete seams onto the block and finish the partial seam at the end. See Partial Seams (below) for details.

PARTIAL SEAMS

1. Lay out the center and border rectangles to form a square.

2. Sew the first rectangle onto the center block partway, backstitch and leave the remainder unsewn.

Partial first seam sewn partway

3. Press the sewn part of the seam away from the center. Add a border rectangle to the sewn side of the unit.

Second rectangle sewn to unit.

4. Add the other 2 border rectangles to the center unit.

5. Finish sewing the first, partial seam to complete the block.

Completing the partial seam block

how to know when it's finished

Take plenty of photos as you are composing your design. It may be a good idea to save them in a folder or print them out to paste in a design journal so you can keep a record of what you have done. Sometimes there are good ideas that didn't work in one project that might work in another.

When I think the design is complete, I often step away from it on the design wall for a few hours or a day, then come back and look at it with fresh eyes.

Here are a few questions to ask yourself:

Do I have interesting lines and shapes? If not, my composition may not be as dynamic as I would like.

Are my color values falling where I want them? Look at your design with a black and white filter on your phone or camera to see where the lights and darks are without regard to the actual color. Sometimes this allows you to see areas that are visually muddy or otherwise need improvement.

Do I have a rhythm to my colors and shapes? Repeating the same or similar colors or shapes in different areas of the quilt can help to create visual texture and move the eye effectively around the design.

Is my composition predictable to the eye? Have I added a pop of color contrast in several places in the quilt? Could I turn one or more of the blocks to create a more striking shape?

Photo by Cindy Grisdela

guided exercises

Guided exercises are intended to give you some ideas for putting your blocks together. They're not patterns, exactly, because I think Improv patterns are a contradiction, but some measurements and guidelines that you can use to get started on your project or to make changes to a project that isn't working for you.

One exercise focuses on using leftover elements to create a new design, as I did with *Baby Blues* (page 50). You will likely have pizza shapes and background pieces with various bites taken out of them, and it's fun to use those limitations to challenge your creativity. The color palette is already chosen, so you just have to decide if you have enough pieces and parts to make an interesting composition, or if you have scraps to add to make it better.

The other exercise takes a completely different approach to freehand curves to create an improv medallion composition. Medallion quilts have been popular in traditional quiltmaking at least partly because they give the artist a way to experiment with different shapes in a structured format. Why not try it with an improv approach?

Curves Around, ˝55 × 55˝, 2025

using leftovers

Spring Blooms by Cindy Grisdela, 43″ × 15″, 2025

A table runner or narrow wall hanging can be a fast gift or a fun way to play with a color palette that you enjoyed from a larger design.

Leftover shapes
Photo by Cindy Grisdela

I designed *Spring Blooms* (above) from a set of leftover shapes from another project. With just three large blocks, it goes together quickly.

I call the shape that has two pizzas cut from opposite corners the dog bone shape, because that's what it reminds me of. Starting from the center using that shape, instead of from a corner, allows you to try a new way of constructing your blocks.

1. Arrange your shapes on the design wall.

2. Choose the center shape to start with and play with arranging the leftover pizza shapes to see which ones work best.

3. Decide if you need to add another element, or perhaps a print for contrast.

Partially sewn leftover elements with dog bone shape
Photo by Cindy Grisdela

In this example, I added pink and green wonky triangles and skinny lines cut from a low-volume black and white print for a pop, plus a striped inset that was left over from a project with a similar color palette. It's okay to add to the leftovers to make a more compelling composition if needed.

4. Sew the curves and additional elements if you are using them to either side of the center shape.

Sewn block with leftovers

Photo by Cindy Grisdela

Sewn block two

Photo by Cindy Grisdela

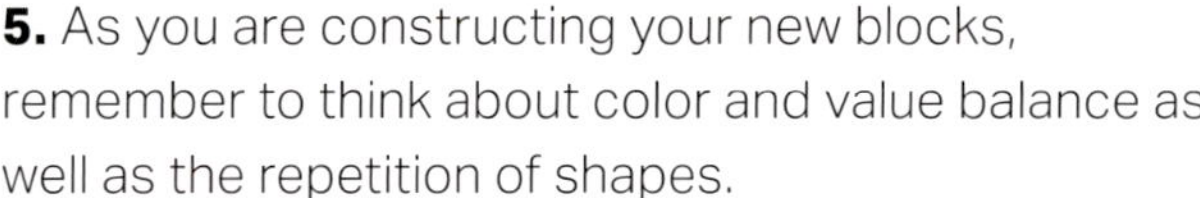

5. As you are constructing your new blocks, remember to think about color and value balance as well as the repetition of shapes.

Bright spring colors like hot pink, orange, and green in a variety of values set the color tone, while a dull gold and dull pear green keep it from being too sugary. The low-volume black and white prints in the skinny lines add a welcome contrast, and I bound the piece with the same fabric because as a table runner, it will be used instead of hanging on the wall.

I used the wonky triangles and fried egg curves in two of the blocks for balance. Those blocks also contain striped insets. The third block has plain insets to help pull it all together.

The three blocks making up the *Spring Blooms* (page 57) table runner are all the same height, 15″, but they are different widths, which sometimes happens when you construct from the center out. The blocks tend to be more rectangular than square. For this project, it didn't make a difference to me as long as they fit together in height.

Sewn block three

Photo by Cindy Grisdela

Raspberry Swirl by Cindy Grisdela, 24″ × 24″, 2025

If you have enough leftover shapes for four blocks, you can put them together into a small wall hanging or table mat. *Raspberry Swirl* (above) was created from elements left over from the design of *Any Which Way* (page 39). I had two dog bone shapes and two squares with one bite taken out of them, plus a wonky triangle curve, some Angled Stripes, and quite a few curve shapes. Using those elements plus a few scraps from the first project, I put together four blocks that incorporated a variety of elements, including pieced insets, wonky triangles, and a fried egg curve.

Balance in the elements and shapes is important in designing a smaller quilt like this one, so the two wonky triangle curves are offset on either side of the block and there are variations in the curves in the center to keep them from being too predictable. The block with the wide purple and coral red inset element is turned so it faces in a different direction than the other three blocks to avoid too much visual weight in the center. Free motion stitching using different motifs in the shapes adds texture and visual interest.

Most of the quilts in this book are a series of blocks puzzled together in different ways. What if we took a look at another way to use freehand curves? Medallion quilts are often thought of as a traditional construction, but there's no reason we can't use Improv techniques to create one.

medallion composition

I had some leftover pizza shapes and other elements from making the technique demo blocks and I put them up on the design wall to see where they would take me. Leftover elements are a little bit like sourdough starter—you can use them to create something entirely different.

I added several print fabrics into the mix from e bond's fabric lines (Free Spirit Fabrics) to add texture and contrast.

Design wall leftovers
Photo by Cindy Grisdela

Curves Around (page 65) is made medallion style from a Four-Patch block of freehand curves, a round of Improv blocks with Insets and Improv Curves, a round of Curved Stripes, and a round of Angled Stripes, and smaller freehand curve blocks. I use these elements frequently in my work, and detailed explanations of the techniques can be found in my other books, *Artful Improv* and *Adventures in Improv Quilts*. I have included general instructions below.

Medallion Center
Photo by Cindy Grisdela

MEDALLION CENTER

The center block is made up of four freehand curve blocks using basic curves, insets, Belly Curves, Fried Egg Curves, Wonky Triangles, and one confetti pop element. After trimming, the block ended up being 23″ square, instead of 24″. That sometimes happens, and there are options to deal with it, because it's not a number that is easily divisible for the next round. One option is to add a narrow border to make it the right size. A 1″-wide strip added as a border on all four sides would make up the difference, including seam allowances.

But I decided to try to make the block work as is.

ROUND ONE

For the corners of the first round corners, I used four Improv Curves.

Improv Curves

1. Cut an 8″ × 8″ square from each of 4 fabrics that coordinate with your palette.

2. Stack the fabrics in a pleasing order right sides up.

3. Cut 3 curves through all 4 layers. In my quilt, 2 curves are cut from 1 corner and 1 from the opposite corner.

4. Lay the block stack out so the 2 curves are on the lower left. Shuffle the block.

5. Leave the lower left pizza stack the way it is. Moving right, take the top fabric from the second curve and put it on the bottom of the stack. The top 2 fabrics from the dog bone shape go on the bottom, and the top 3 fabrics from the opposite pizza go to the bottom. There should be a different fabric in each section of the block stack.

6. Sew the blocks together and trim to 6½″ × 6½″ square.

Place the finished blocks on the four corners of the center.

Medallion with round one corners

Photo by Cindy Grisdela

Giving the Eye a Place to Rest
Medallion-style quilts can be quite busy. If that concerns you, it's important to think about areas of negative space in some of the border rounds to give a resting space for the eye.

The sides of the first round are made up of small pieced improv blocks with borders and insets alternating with plain rectangles with insets. The open space in the block borders and the rectangles provide negative space that gives a resting area for the eye in the composition. To keep the palette from being too matchy, I used a soft gray value for the block borders and the rectangles, which sets off the center and provides visual texture.

The improv blocks are 6½″ × 6½″ square to match the size of the Improv Curves on the corners. Because the center measured 23″ instead of 24″, 4 blocks would be too many. I could have cut them down to fit, but I wanted to make sure there was enough negative space to give this round a calming effect.

To solve the problem, I used 3 Improv Blocks 6½″ × 6½″ and 2 rectangles 3″ × 6½″ with an inset on each side. The insets in the blocks and in the rectangles are offset, which adds repetition and variety to the design.

IMPROV BLOCKS

1. Use scraps to make tiny 3″ × 3″ square compositions. Each has a small piece of the black print for consistency.

2. Cut 2½″-wide strips of background fabric and narrow 1″–1¼″-wide strips of contrasting fabric for insets. The inset fabrics can be all the same color or several colors with similar values. In my quilt I used several values of hot pink and red orange.

Improv Block with Strips deconstructed

3. Decide where the insets will go on the background fabric. They can be on 2, 3, or all 4 sides. Cut openings in the background and sew insets into those spaces.

4. Sew the inset rectangles to the center block. I usually add them clockwise.

5. Cut 3″-wide strips of background fabric for the rectangles with insets.

6. Make 8 spacer blocks with 1 inset each.

Improv blocks finished with spacer block

7. Lay the Improv Blocks out next to the center, 1 on each end and 1 in the middle. Place the spacer rectangles in the 2 empty spaces to fill out each side.

8. Each rectangle has 1 inset to keep the design from getting too busy. Decide where the inset will go in relation to the other blocks and sew it in.

Medallion with round 1 Improv Curve corners and Improv Blocks with spacers

Photo by Cindy Grisdela

9. Sew the Improv Blocks to the rectangles to create a side strip.

10. Sew these strips to each side of the center.

11. Sew the top and bottom strips to the corner curves, then sew those units to the center unit.

ROUND TWO

Round two is a Curved Stripe border. Choose two fabrics that have a high degree of contrast so your curve will show. I used a red print and a very pale pink.

Curved Stripes

1. Cut a strip 2½″ × width of fabric from each fabric.

2. Lay the strips out on the cutting mat *right sides up*. Overlap 1 strip over the other on the long sides about 1″. Cut a gently curving line through both layers with your rotary cutter. Think about creating hills and valleys that aren't too steep.

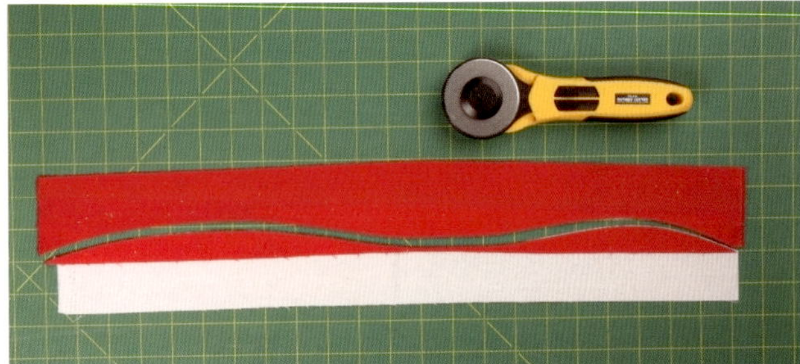

Curved stripes with overlap and cut curve

3. Remove the narrow excess strips from each fabric and note that your curves fit together exactly.

4. Sew the curves together on the long edge right sides together. It will look like it won't fit. I don't pin these curves because they change direction. Just ease the curve together gently as you sew, stopping if needed to realign the raw edges. A ¼″ seam allowance is ideal, but your aim should be a smooth curve, so if there are places that it's a little narrower, don't worry about it.

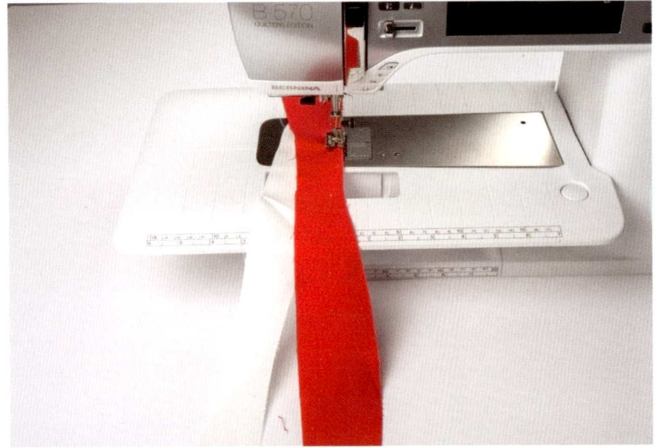

Sewing curves

5. Trim the stripes if needed to even up the long raw edges.

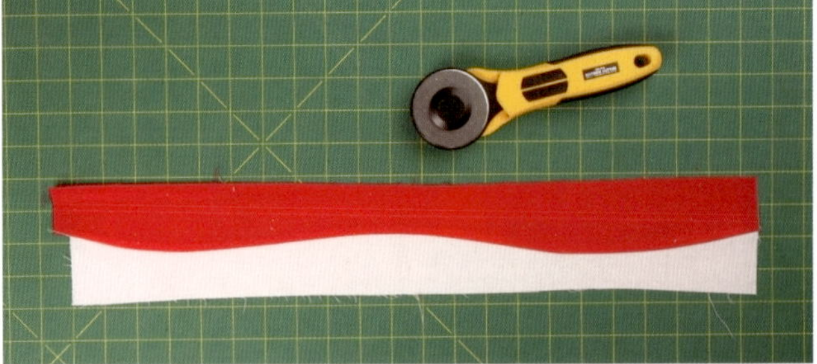

Curved Stripe

6. Sew the stripes onto the center unit using partial seaming (page 53).

Medallion with round two Curved Stripes border

Photo by Cindy Grisdela

ROUND THREE

The final round is made up of Angled Stripe units with four small freehand curves in the corners. I added the curves in the corners of rounds one and three to stick with the curve theme, but you could change them to any square block or continue the border up into the corners. I like interrupting the border because it adds new lines and shapes that draw the eye around the design. The curves also help to add movement to the piece.

Angled Stripe Units

Choose 5–7 fabrics for each set of 9″ × 11″ rectangles. For this border I used 3 sets of 7 fabrics for round three. See Angled Stripes (page 43) for instructions to cut the angles, shuffle the stacks, and sew the sets together.

Trim the blocks to 8½″ × 8½″ square. Sew them into strips so the stripes face into the center unit. Lay them out next to the center unit to see how they fit. Depending on how many fabrics you use and the angle of your cuts, you may need another set, or you may add coping strips to your stripes.

The corner curve blocks are 8½″ × 8½″ squares made using your favorite techniques from the Techniques chapter (page 20). Because these blocks are smaller, you will start out with 10″ squares and probably use fewer elements than in the larger blocks.

Make four corner curve blocks.

Sew the striped units and the corner blocks to the center unit.

Curves Around Medallion

add texture with quilting

Once your quilt top is complete, how do you quilt it?

I started out my quilting journey as a machine piecer and hand quilter making mostly traditional quilts. But the quilt tops started to pile up and the list of quilts I wanted to make kept getting longer and longer, and I realized I would have to learn to use my machine to create the finishing texture in my work to get through it all.

There are multiple ways to add stitching to hold the three layers of your quilt together and add interesting texture and dimension to your work. The two I use most often are lines with a walking foot and free motion stitching with a darning or hopping foot.

'70s Serpentine by Cindy Grisdela, 54″ × 54″, 2025

walking foot

The easiest way to add the stitching texture to a quilt is using a walking foot. The walking foot is an extra attachment on most machines that feeds the fabric evenly on both the top and the bottom of the quilt. It's a worthwhile investment if you do a lot of your own quilting. That even feed helps to minimize tucks, puckers, and pleats on the back side of the quilt, but it's a good idea to check every so often to make sure the back looks as good as the front.

IRREGULAR STRAIGHT LINES

To make straight lines of stitching on your quilt, decide if you want the lines to be vertical or horizontal. Start in the middle of the quilt and stitch the first line. If a seam line is available, I use that to begin. If not, I use a length of blue painter's tape to establish the first line.

Once you've made that first pass, remove the painter's tape if you used it, and use the edge of the walking foot on the previous stitching line to stitch parallel lines to the left and right of center. My walking foot is about ½″ wide, so that's the spacing that I automatically get.

To make the spacing irregular, go back over the quilt and stitch in between some of the ½″ lines, but not all of them, making the texture more interesting.

Fiesta detail of straight line quilting

WAVY LINES

You can also use the walking foot to create wavy lines, either horizontally or vertically, or both. I suggest practicing this on a smaller piece first before trying it on a large quilt.

Start in the middle of the quilt as before. Using a seam line or painter's tape as a guide, stitch a gently waving line from one end of the quilt to the other. Think about hills and valleys to create an undulating line. Remove the tape if you used it and stitch another wavy line to the left or right of the first. I usually make the second line form a rough hourglass shape compared with the first line.

If you wish, echo some of the lines to create a new shape. Continue until the entire quilt is stitched.

Twist and Shout detail with wavy line stitching

If the wavy lines are vertical, you can go back and add horizontal lines that cross the original lines for an interesting crosshatching texture. I recommend trying this on a small piece first. To stitch crosshatched wavy lines on *Spring Blooms* (below), I stitched the shorter horizontal lines first, then the longer vertical lines. In addition, I left some space in the middle of the piece and on either side where I didn't add the vertical lines.

Spring Blooms

Drawing with hatched wavy lines

Spring Blooms thatched wavy line stitching detail

free-motion quilting

These freehand curve blocks are a great time to experiment with free-motion quilting. I like to stitch a different motif in each curved area, matching the thread to the fabric as much as possible. While this results in a lot of stopping and starting, the results can be spectacular.

You'll need an open- or closed-toe darning or hopping foot for free-motion quilting and the ability to lower your feed dogs. The foot doesn't put any pressure on the quilt top and the lowered feed dogs remove pressure on the underside of your work, so all the machine is doing is making the needle go up and down. This allows you to stitch in any direction to create the motifs you want.

'70s Serpentine (right), *Supernova* (page 14), and *Baby Blues* (page 50) are all stitched in this way.

'70s Serpentine by Cindy Grisdela 54″ × 54″, 2025

Begin roughly in the center of the quilt. Stitch motifs in two or three blocks, changing the threads as you go. Once those blocks are done, it's often possible to group the colors. Look for curves that are the same color and touching an area that has already been quilted so you can stitch several curved shapes of the same color before needing to change the thread.

'70s Serpentine free-motion stitching detail

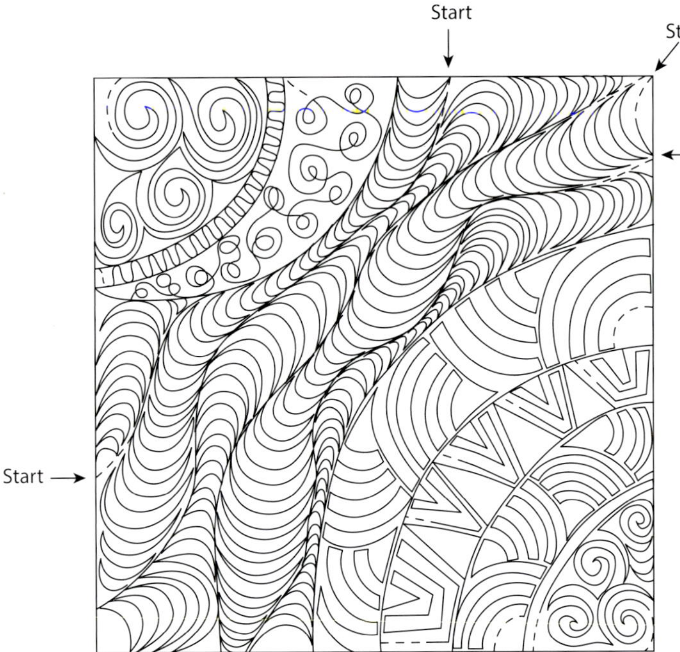

Motifs in *'70s Serpentine* block

Let's use one block from *'70s Serpentine* as an example (page 69).

The brown pizza shape in the upper right is stitched with nesting spirals, the striped curve underneath it has lozenges, and the green curve underneath has open spirals.

Nesting spirals are an example of a closed spiral shape where the stitching lines don't cross. Begin on one edge of the shape and stitch a spiral into the center, leaving room to pivot and come back out. To create the nesting effect, echo the spiral until the stitching line touches another element of the design, either the edge of the shape or another line of stitching. Then echo back to touch an element on the other side and begin another spiral.

Lozenges are a good motif to use in narrow curve areas. Start at one end of the curve and stitch vertical lines up and down the shape, creating a curve at the top and the bottom.

Open spirals have stitching lines that do cross each other. Stitch a spiral shape into the center and then pivot and shoot the stitching line out across the lines of stitching to create a new spiral.

In the yellow shape I call the dog bone, I used stacked waves to create a flowing effect.

Nesting spirals, lozenges, and open spirals

'70s Serpentine wave stitching on the machine

Photo by Cindy Grisdela

Stacked waves take a little time to stitch, but the effect can be stunning. See the stitching example (right) for a look at how the waves are created.

First stitch several gently curving lines about 1″–2″ apart from one end of the dog bone shape to the other on the long side of the shape. These are the lines you will use as registration lines to divide and stack your wave. You can do this either with a walking foot or with your free motion darning foot because the lines really won't show much. Starting in the middle of the shape, stitch crescent shapes between two lines, bouncing from one line to the other. When you get to the end, move to the next set of lines and stitch crescent shapes going the other direction.

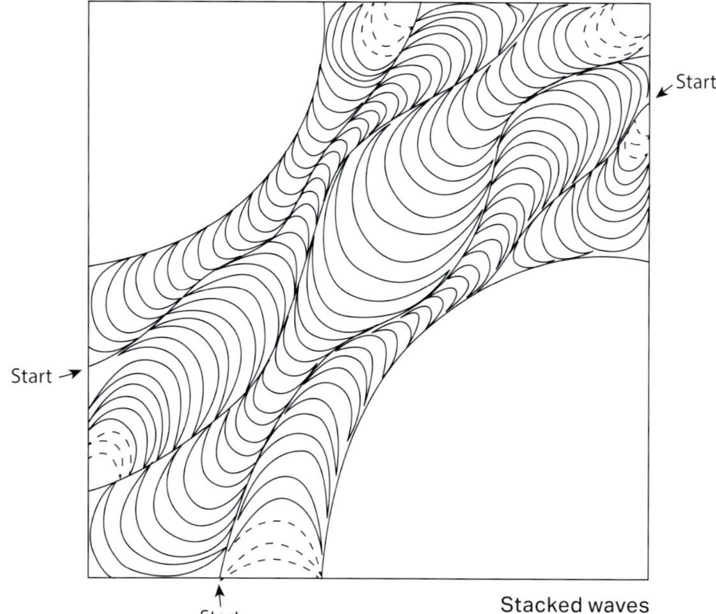

Stacked waves

The light blue curve has fans, while the triangle curve has chevrons stitched in straight lines in the background of the triangles. You can use a walking foot here or your free-motion foot, depending on how organic you want the lines to be. I used my free-motion foot. I left the triangle shapes unquilted so they would pop forward visually in the design.

Fans are a versatile motif that work well in either a contained space like these blocks or as an overall design. Begin at one edge of the shape and stitch a curve from one side to the other. Pivot and stitch three or four stitches, then pivot again and echo the curve shape you just stitched to the other side. Repeat the echo two or three times and then start another fan.

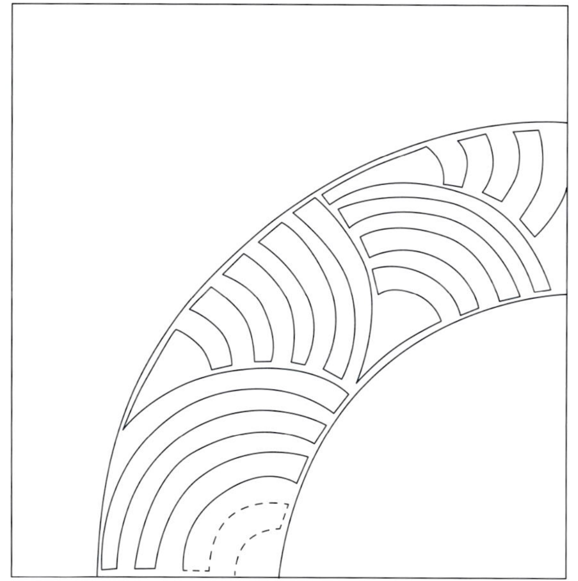
Fans

I divided the coral red pizza shape in the lower right into two sections with a double curved line in the middle of the shape. The upper section is stitched with fans and the lower section with nesting spirals. I did this in several places where the pizza shape was on the large side to make it more interesting.

This method takes a little more time than an allover walking foot design, but it's much more fun to stitch and to look at once it's finished.

'70s Serpentine block detail with various stitching motifs

Open square spirals

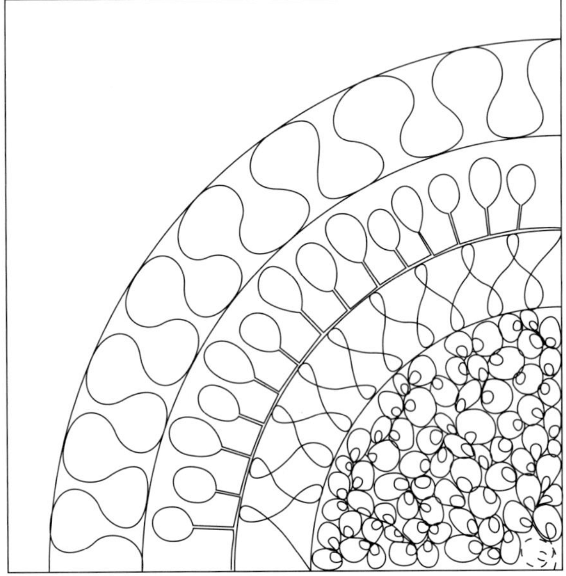

Lollipop trees, lazy S, ribbon candy, pebble variation

Other blocks in *'70's Serpentine* have different motifs to try.

In the blocks with striped pizza insets I used **open square spirals** with a Mid-Century Modern feel. Begin at one edge of the shape to be filled. Stitch a square spiral into the center, then pivot and stitch a line going outside the spiral. You can add a rectangle inside the spiral first if you like that look. The new line starts another spiral. The squares don't have to line up, and sometimes it's more striking if they don't. I left the striped inset unquilted.

Other motifs I used in this quilt are lollipop trees, lazy S's, ribbon candy, and a pebble variation.

Lollipop trees are stitched from the bottom of the curve. Start at one edge of the curve to be filled and stitch a few stitches right along the bottom edge. Pivot and stitch a stem, then a round or oval shape on top of the stem. Retrace your stitching down the stem and stitch a few more stitches at the bottom of the curve to make room to create another tree. Continue until the curve is filled. I like to stagger the "trees" so they aren't all in the same line.

The **lazy S** motif works well to cover a busy area in the block. I used it on several of the curves in *'70s Serpentine* that are made up of stripes. Start at one bottom edge of the curve and stitch a diagonal line up to the top of the curve. Make a small oval at the top stitching counterclockwise, then stitch another diagonal line down to the bottom of the curve. Make another small oval going clockwise. The S shapes can be either close together or farther apart. Experiment with what looks best to you.

Ribbon candy is relatively fast to stitch and covers a curve easily. Start at one edge of the curve and stitch a gently curving line that bellies out near the top. Continue stitching the rounded shape at the top of the curve and around the other side. Bring the stitching line toward the first curve you created, forming an hourglass type shape, then round it out at the bottom of the curve and repeat.

Pebbles are a popular motif with many applications. Many times, students feel it's difficult to get the pebbles consistent. This variation helps to draw attention away from the individual pebble and toward the texture being created. Begin at one edge of the shape to be filled, stitch a round or oval pebble shape, then stitch a smaller round or oval shape inside the pebble. Come out of the shape and stitch another pebble with a circle or oval inside it. Continue to fill the space, retracing your stitches as needed to get to another area to make new pebbles. Try to vary the size and shape of your pebbles as you stitch.

Often I choose motifs for specific areas in the design as I'm working and repeat them for consistency. In *'70s Serpentine* (page 69), I wasn't sure what to stitch in the dog bone shape, so there are two blocks near the center with an echoing line motif. That didn't work as well as I had hoped, so I changed the motif to the stacked waves, which worked much better. I decided to leave the first blocks the way they were instead of ripping that part out.

All of the wonky triangles are stitched with the straight-line chevrons, the triangle shapes are left unquilted, and many of the fried egg shapes are stitched with fans. This way I don't have to make quite as many decisions as I'm working on a large piece. You might decide to try it another way.

Free-motion stitching is a hand process, despite the fact you're using a machine to do the work. You are driving the shapes as you go, drawing them with your needle and thread. It takes practice to get good at it, but you can make small projects with different motifs to do that. I like to suggest that students make a set of place mats with a different motif on each one. Or you could make a table runner like *Spring Blooms* (page 57) and try different motifs in each curved area. With only three blocks, you will have something to show for your work in no time.

Another way to practice is to decide on a few motifs you'd like to get better at and draw them on paper. That allows you to get your hand and your brain aligned on what the shape will look like and makes it easier to stitch at the machine.

Try not to focus on each individual stitch and whether it is the same length as the ones around it. Focus instead on the texture you are adding to your project. That's what viewers will see when it's all finished—any bobbles or inconsistencies will be part of the charm.

Don't forget to sign your work! Stitching your name may be the easiest free motion you can do because you sign your name all the time and you have the muscle memory to do it well.

Free motion signature on *Spring Blooms*

Once you have pieced your quilt and stitched the texture onto it, it's time to decide how to finish the edges. Traditionally, quilts were finished with a bound edge, typically a double fold of fabric that either matched or contrasted with the body of the quilt to stabilize the edges under heavy use. But that's not the only way to finish the edge of a quilt.

I use facings to finish the edges of my larger quilts. A facing is like a fabric frame that is sewn onto a finished wall hanging to enclose the raw edges. The frame is machine sewn onto the front of the quilt right sides together, then turned to the back and pressed so it doesn't show on the front, and hand stitched in place.

I like to mount my smaller quilts on canvas to make them stand out on the wall. If you like working small to explore new ideas, mounting on canvas is an easy way to present the work without having people ask you why you're putting a potholder on the wall!

Let's take a look at my process for each of these options.

Raspberry Swirl by Cindy Grisdela, 24″ × 24″, 2025

frame facing

I prefer facings on my quilts because they are meant to be decorative art to hang on the wall, rather than functional pieces for a bed. Bindings are generally used in traditional functional quilts beca use they provide a double edge on the quilt that will wear longer.

But for a wall quilt, a facing works better to present my work as art. The design comes all the way out to the edges of the quilt, without the distraction of another line in the binding around the outside. A facing is a dressmaking tool, often used on the openings of a blouse, for example. In quiltmaking, a facing is used to enclose the raw edges of the quilt and help the outer seam lie flat. To face a quilt using this method, you will create a custom frame for the piece out of 2½″-wide strips. The frame is sewn to the raw edges of the quilt, right sides together, and folded to the back so there is a crisp edge to the design.

1. Quilt the quilt as desired, stitching through top, batting, and backing. Trim the edges evenly.

Spring Crocus **quilted top**

Photo by Cindy Grisdela

2. Pin the quilt up on a design wall or other surface so you can see all the edges.

3. Cut 2 strips 2½″ × the length of 2 opposite sides of your quilt—I usually start with the right and left sides. Press under ¼″ along one long edge. This edge will go toward the inside of the quilt to be handstitched down at the end.

4. Lay the strips across the 2 opposite sides of the quilt, right sides together, with raw edges even and the fold on the inside away from the edge.

Left/right strips

Photo by Cindy Grisdela

5. Measure the top and bottom sides from the fold of 1 side facing to the fold of the other side facing, then add ½″ for seam allowances on each end. Cut 2 strips this measurement and press under ¼″ on one long edge.

6. On the left side strip, open up the fold in the upper right corner and match the raw edge of the top strip to the raw edge of the open fold. Make sure the left side fold is on the inside and the raw edges match on the sides. This creates 1 corner of the frame.

7. With right sides together, stitch along the open fold line just the width of the top strip, keeping the top side fold closed. Press towards the left side strip.

Spring Crocus with Frame

Photo by Cindy Grisdela

8. Repeat Steps 6 and 7 for the other corners, creating your custom frame.

9. Lay the frame on the quilt, right sides together. Pin and stitch through all layers, with the facing side up. It may help to use a walking foot attachment if you have one. Clip the corners.

10. Turn the facing to the back of the quilt. Use a chopstick or other pointed end to carefully push out the corners. Press the facing to the back so the seam lies flat, using steam if you need it. The seam should lie exactly on the edge so you don't see it from the front.

11. Pin the facing in place and handstitch the folded edges to the back of the quilt.

Spring Crocus back

Spring Crocus by Cindy Grisdela, 20″ × 20″, 2025

pieced backings

Any Which Way Back

I've been quilting for a long time, and I have a lot of print fabrics that I am unlikely to use on the fronts of my quilts anymore. So, I use them on the back.

Generally, I choose fabrics from my stash that are similar in color or feel to the front. They may have irregular edges or bites taken out of them from being used in other projects. I cut them into squares or rectangles and piece them in a pleasing order to create a slab of fabric big enough to be a backing. I've even used 100% cotton napkins that were too ragged on the edges to use for that purpose anymore.

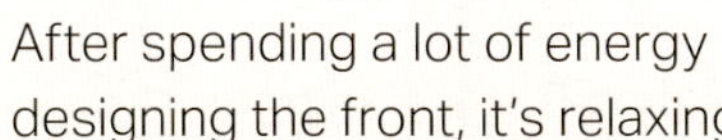

After spending a lot of energy designing the front, it's relaxing to just cut and sew chunks of fabric together for the back without having to think too much about color and placement. And it keeps the fabric I'm not using out of the landfill.

mounting on canvas

Mounting on canvas is an easy, economical way to present smaller quilts as art. The canvas background gives these quiltlets more presence on the wall and they are easy to hang from a wire on the back—no need to bother with sleeves, slats and multiple nails.

Pre-stretched canvases come in standard sizes. My most popular sizes are 8″ × 8″, 12″ × 12″, 16″ × 20″, and 20″ × 20″. It's certainly possible to use larger sizes, but they become somewhat unwieldy for me to transport, so I stick to these four. I like the ones that are 1½″ deep. The canvases are readily available from art supply stores.

Plan the Finished Size

Because the finished size of the canvas is set, you need to plan the quilt size ahead of time if you want to use this method. My preference is to have the quilted but unfinished quilt be ¼″ larger than the size of the canvas. For example, a quilt intended for a 12″ square canvas should be 12¼″ × 12¼″ square after quilting and trimming. Then, after sewing a back on to enclose the raw edges, the final size will be 11¾″ × 11¾″. This gives you a very small reveal of the black canvas from the front. I found that trying to make the quilt fit exactly onto the canvas was frustrating—there was always some little piece that stuck out over the edge.

To get started, create your quilt in the usual way, sandwich it with batting and backing, and quilt it through all three layers. Then follow these steps to mount it on canvas.

Mounting on canvas materials

Photo by Cindy Grisdela

1. Use a foam brush to paint the canvas with black acrylic paint on all 4 sides and about 1½″ into the front. There's no need to paint the whole canvas because it will be covered up with the quilt. Black works for me because it doesn't compete with the quilt on the front. I experimented with using different colors in the beginning and decided that sticking with a consistent black canvas was the best choice.

2. Trim the quilted but still raw-edged quilt to be ¼″ larger than the canvas size. (See Plan the Finished Size, page 77)

3. To enclose the edges of your work, cut a piece of black fabric the same size as the quilt. Again, I use black fabric regardless of the color of the quilt, because it will blend in to the black paint on the canvas without distracting from the quilt itself.

4. With right sides together, stitch all the way around the edges of the quilt using a ¼″ seam allowance.

5. Carefully cut a small slit in the black fabric. Be careful not to cut the quilt! Clip the corners, and turn the work right side out, like a pillowcase.

6. Press the piece carefully to make sharp edges all around.

7. Adhere the quilt to the canvas by running a thin line of gel medium along the outer edges of the canvas and then make lazy "S" shapes in the middle of the canvas. Be careful to use a thin layer—it will hold the quilt on just fine without soaking through to the quilt.

8. Center the finished quilt carefully onto the canvas. Check to make sure there is gel medium on the corners and add another drop if necessary.

9. Press the quilt gently onto the canvas and carefully wipe away any gel medium that seeps out along the edges. Gel medium doesn't dry clear, so you don't want any to show.

10. Place a layer of wax paper over the quilt and weigh it down with books for a few hours or overnight.

11. When the piece is dry, sign the back, attach hooks and wire, and your quiltlet is ready to hang on the wall!

Early Dawn by Cindy Grisdela, 12″ × 12″, 2025

Small quiltlet mounted on canvas

It is possible to remove the quilt from the canvas without harm, although the facing will have to be replaced. I have had to do this for a variety of reasons, and even after several years, the bond is strong, and the quilt is fine.

Scrap jars with mounted 12″ × 12″ quiltlets in my studio.

Photo by Cindy Grisdela

If for some reason you aren't comfortable with adhering the gel medium directly to the back of your quilt, another option is to tack your faced quilt to a piece of black felt with hand stitching and then adhere the felt to the canvas as described above. Cut the felt just slightly smaller than the finished quilt.

There are many different methods to attach quilts to canvas, including stitching, adding a background, and wrapping around the canvas, or using hook-and-loop tape, but this is the way I do it and I've been happy with the results.

student gallery

As a teacher, I want to give my students the confidence to explore their own creativity and bring their designs to the world. I understand that I'm unlikely to make every student I teach an Improv artist, but my hope is to give them some tools and ideas that they can apply to their own artistic practice.

Teaching brings me joy and I love sharing my passion for color and design with students in person and online, and of course through my books.

I'm grateful to these students for sharing their work for this book—Angela Gubler, Sherrill Ash, Candi Lennox, Nina Clotfelter, and Linda Hungerford.

An Unexpected Consequence by Angela Gubler, 37″ × 38″, 2024

An Unexpected Consequence by Angela Gubler, 37″ × 38″, 2024

Angela made some of her curved blocks with unique insets. She also added black and white cross blocks and Improv-pieced blocks to her composition. She showcases another way to use freehand curves in an original composition.

Infinity Fractured by Sherrill Ash, 32″ × 35″, 2024

Sherrill used a controlled color palette of red, white, blue, and gray, plus several prints and stripes in her composition. The setting is a cog structure with no complete circles. She used coping curves (page 48) cutting across some of her blocks to great effect.

Spin Cycle by Candi Lennox, 50˝ × 51˝, 2023

Candi started her composition with blue, green, and orange in a class with me, then added yellow once the design evolved on her design wall at home. She has a variety of values of each color in the quilt, plus white. The way she cut some of her curves with lines that have bellies and waves, and the colors she used adds a lot of energy to the finished piece.

Radiant Ripples by Nina Clotfelter, 38″ × 39″, 2025

Nina used a red, pink, purple, and gray color palette with a pop of yellow for *Radiant Ripples* (above). Her setting is also a cog structure with no full circles, successfully drawing the eye around the design. Free-motion quilting using many different motifs adds texture and dimension to the overall design.

Party Time! by Linda Hungerford, 64″ × 69″, 2025

Photo by Linda Hungerford

Linda combined Improv Curves with freehand curves to create a boldly-energetic composition using several values of orange, red, purple, and burgundy for *Party Time!*. She used white and turquoise as pops of contrast in the center, drawing the eye effectively around the design. Triangles in different sizes and confetti dots dance around the perimeter of the quilt. Some dots are pieced and some are appliqued. A variety of motifs using a walking foot and free-motion quilting create texture and activate the design.

about the author

Cindy Grisdela has been intrigued by color, line, and shape most of her life. She learned to sew from her mother as a child and took many art classes in high school. In college she majored in art history and dove deeply into the work of modern painters. Henri Matisse, Paul Klee, Joan Miró, Robert Diebenkorn, Georgia O'Keeffe, and Robert and Sonia Delaunay are particular favorites.

There weren't any quilters in her family, so Cindy made clothing as a teenager and young adult. She discovered quilting from an article in a women's magazine when she was in college and was almost immediately hooked on the idea of creating with fabric and thread.

Cindy is known now for her fearless approach to color, but it wasn't always that way. In those early days as a quilter, she made traditional quilts from patterns and was intimidated by color, so she made a lot of blue quilts! But gradually she became more comfortable with putting colors together in pleasing combinations and started challenging herself to use colors that weren't as comfortable, like red, orange, yellow and even brown. Even if they don't turn out to be her new favorite colors, she learns from each color experiment.

Working with fabric like it was paint, Cindy creates dynamic contemporary compositions, cutting the shapes out freehand without a pattern or template and sewing them together with the sewing machine. There are no rules in this process, except the guidelines she gives herself as she works to give structure to the project. Often the original idea goes through several variations as the composition evolves and Cindy responds to the lines and shapes taking form on the design wall.

Neon Fizz II by Cindy Grisdela, 25″ × 25″, 2021.

Although her work is abstract, Cindy finds inspiration in all kinds of places, from the colors on the lake outside her studio window to interesting combinations of shapes in buildings and cityscapes to the colors and shapes in paintings. She has even made a couple of quilts inspired by the designs on favorite sweaters! She takes lots of pictures on her phone when she's out, especially when she travels to a new place, trying to look at her surroundings with the eye of an artist. You never know where inspiration will come from in new colors, shapes and textures.

There's a reason Cindy chose to create her art in fabric and thread rather than paint, and that's the opportunity to add texture to her compositions with the stitching lines.

Feeling that texture of the stitching lines coming to life under her fingers is one of the things that drew her to creating in this way and keeps her excited about going into the studio every day.

Cindy is a full-time artist and teacher. She travels all over the country giving lectures and workshops on color and Improv Design, as well as teaching and lecturing online. She has appeared on *Quilting Arts TV* and *The Quilt Show* and she is a juried artist member of Studio Art Quilt Associates. Cindy is also an instructor at the interactive platform Creative Spark Online Learning by C&T Publishing.

Visit Cindy online at cindygrisdela.com or follow her on Instagram @cindygrisdelaquilts, or on Facebook /cindygrisdelaquilts

RESOURCES

Here are a few of my favorite books on quilting, design, and color. Some may be out of print and available at the public library or used book stores.

Adventures in Design, by Joen Wolfrom (C&T Publishing)

An Eye for Color, by Olga Gutierrez de la Roza (Harper)

At Play in the Garden of Stitch, by Paula Kovarik (Yellowbrick Studio Press)

Gee's Bend: the Architecture of the Quilt, by Paul Arnett, et al. (Tinwood Books)

Improv Quilting: Dancing with the Wall, by Irene Roderick (Krause Craft)

All books by Gwen Marston

Improvisational Quilts, by Nancy Crow (C&T Publishing)

Walk: Master Machine Quilting with your Walking Foot, by Jacquie Gering (Lucky Spool Media)

CREATIVE SPARK

ONLINE LEARNING

Quilting courses to become an expert quilter...

From their studio to yours, Creative Spark instructors are teaching you how to create and become a master of your craft. So not only do you get a look inside their creative space, you also get to be a part of engaging courses that would typically be a one or multi-day workshop from the comfort of your home.

Creative Spark is not your one-size-fits-all online learning experience. We welcome you to be who you are, share, create, and belong.

Scan for a gift from us!

creativespark.ctpub.com